46 DAYS

The Story of Frank Giannino's Record-Breaking Run Across America

by

KEVIN GLEASON

Edit, design and layout by Beth Quinn

ISBN: 978-1533218506

For a Pair of Angelic Mothers

Josephine Giacalone, Frank's step-mom (now 90), the unsung hero and perhaps toughest crew member. Without her, there wouldn't have been a record-breaking run.

And Eileen Gleason, who left behind her unforgettable touch and flair for storytelling before leaving us too soon.

- Frank and Kevin

Contents

Foreword

Are there really people who *have* to run across the United States?

The short and perhaps unbelievable answer is yes.

But why? Why would anyone be driven to go so far?

Frank Giannino ran from San Francisco to New York, not just once but twice, and he still holds the world record for his second crossing in 1980 when he was just twenty-eight years old.

In short, he's the guy to beat. Setting that record meant spending just over forty-six days on the road, an average of almost sixty-seven miles on foot per day. That pace over that distance is nothing short of remarkable, a benchmark even the most elite distance runners alive today would be lucky to replicate, much less outdo.

Without irony, Frank has called himself a "no-talent ultra-marathoner." He insists that his record is "soft." Yet it's now been more than three decades, and no one has come close to eclipsing it. I tried. So have others.

The truth? Frank's run was historic, gargantuan, a feat to be marveled at and respected.

But this question of why … In *46 Days,* you get Frank's honest, unembellished, raw story, the who and how and whatever the hell for. It reveals the physical toll of this feat (the daily mileage Frank logged is mind-boggling), the events and emotions that led him to undertake it, and the effects on those around him before, during, and after he did so.

More poignant, this book also shares the mundane obstacles Frank had to overcome – the kind of pains and problems familiar to everyone: romantic heartache, apparent physical limitations, self-doubt, disappointment and despair.

Marshall Ulrich

Yet, ultimately, it shows us how, with support from family and friends, to find pleasure and fulfillment by setting and reaching a cherished "impossible" goal. It's about time the full saga of his incredible run was told, including not only the grandiose vision and superhuman grit it took to pull this off, but also the all-too-human trials along the way to its accomplishment. To me, Frank will always be King of the Road.

Marshall Ulrich
With Heather Ulrich

Author's Note: Marshall has conquered seemingly impossible endurance obstacles, including more than one hundred races averaging at least 125 miles. Yet he considers his most difficult challenge trying to break Frank's record in Fall 2008. Marshall came short of the mark while setting two masters records by running 3,063.2 miles in 52.5 days, an average of 58.3 miles per day, as chronicled in his book, *Running on Empty*.

1

Why?

Frank Giannino sat on the steps of his motor home in front of San Francisco City Hall moments before the start of his second run across the United States of America. It was Labor Day 1980 with much of San Francisco fast asleep. But Giannino never felt more alive, more in control, more real, applying Vaseline to the balls of his feet and sliding gauze between his toes.

"Mr. Giannini, ABC News, why are you making this run?"

"It's Gi-a-nni-no – with an o," he said smiling. "Call me Frank."

"Okay Frank. Why?"

"Because I like to run."

The answer, at least to runners, is always longer and deeper than that. The answer usually rests somewhere deep inside your soul. But the hard part, sometimes the seemingly impossible part, is finding clarity in why you run long distances, why you run every day or almost every day, why you run through choking heat and Arctic cold and torrential rain and unsightly blizzards and nagging pain and awful sickness, why you run in the dark of morning and night and any time in between with the sole purpose of laying your head on a pillow uniquely satisfied, even victorious, before shutting down the world to sleep.

When you decide to expand your hobby into a 3,000-mile run across the country, sometimes the answer is found years earlier when you discover the depths of critical thinking.

People walk. People run. A lot of people walk and run. A lot of people walk and run long distances.

Very few people run 3,000 miles.

Frank was about to start his 3,000-mile adventure across the country not for the first time, but for the second straight year. He had successfully navigated the distance only sixteen months earlier. But it wasn't good enough. So he was doing it again. He felt as though he had to do it again.

And yet he still wasn't exactly sure why he was doing it again. About all he knew was that he wanted to break the world record for the fastest run across the United States.

He had some clues to what brought him in front of San Francisco City Hall on the first day of September, 1980. It would become the very day when Canadian humanitarian Terry Fox was forced to end his Marathon of Hope run outside of Thunder Bay, Ontario. Fox, his right leg amputated because of cancer, had begun his trek in April in St. John's, Newfoundland, trying to raise $24 million for cancer research, the idea to raise $1 from each of the 24 million residents of Canada. He completed 3,339 miles in 143 days before being forced to stop when the cancer had spread to his lungs.

Frank certainly was inspired by Fox. But Frank's first transcontinental run preceded Fox's journey. Frank's adventures centered on his longing for attention and finishing ahead of the field and ... something else. There had to be something else, something more, even, than a world record.

But what made him seek *this* kind of attention? There would seem to be only so many back slaps and hand claps to make a 3,000-mile run worthwhile. And not all the attention was positive. A decent percentage of folks looked upon such "adventure runs" apathetically, dismissing worthy candidates as odd, if not full-fledged crazy, certainly not heroic or extraordinary. Others in a group known as ultra-marathoners, those dedicated to racing beyond the 26.2-mile marathon distance, were protective of their turf, viewing such non-ultra runners attempting great distances with skepticism if not disbelief.

4

Still others looked upon such runs with curiosity, even dismay, but little else, too busy following bouncing balls and freakishly large athletes who made up leagues with abbreviations familiar to all. NFL, MLB, NBA. Perhaps those folks numbered more than any group, which would explain the almost complete lack of media attention and fan support given runners at different points, even starts and finishes, to almost all transcontinental treks.

What could Frank say at the moment? Even if he knew exactly why he was about to run from San Francisco to New York, he couldn't fit a virtual lifetime of insecurity and disappointment and misery into a thirty-second sound byte.

The pre-run news conference was about to begin on the steps of City Hall. The major networks sent camera crews. There was another film crew from the World of People, a nationally syndicated TV show documenting parts of the run. But this being a holiday and all, or this being a crazy cross-country run and all, there was little depth of coverage or political interest. San Francisco mayor Diane Feinstein was absent, as were other high-ranking city officials, though Fire Chief Andrew C. Casper made it. Casper, born and raised in San Fran, was described by the San Francisco Chronicle as an old-school take-charge boss who rushed to fires in his red chief's car. Perhaps Casper's experience with folks at risk made his presence mandatory.

The slights were appropriate. After all, it was Frank Giannini, err, Giannino. He had spent a good chunk of his twenty-eight years searching for respect, a desperate plea, really, laced with insecurity and its tormenting twin, self-doubt. Why should the theme of this send-off be anything other than a singular search for acceptance and stardom? He figured he would receive ample attention later, after he broke the world record and saw his name in the Guinness Book of World Records.

So the official speaker was the San Francisco Fire Chief and not the mayor or Governor Jerry Brown. Frank wasn't caught up in the festivities anyway. He just wanted to get going. He wanted to get started with the rest of his life.

The obligatory speeches were made. Frank said a few words. He thanked as many people as he could remember who played a critical role in helping him to the starting line. Now it was time to go.

So when the newswoman asked the obligatory "Why" question, Frank took a shortcut.

Because I like to run, he said, that's why.

Finally, still on the steps, Frank and six other runners joining him for the ceremonial start took off at 8:17 a.m.

Four of them planned to be on hand for the duration. There was younger brother John, seventeen, with permission from his school district in Orange County, New York, to delay the start of his senior year, waiting at the bottom steps. John would ride his bicycle most of the route, sometimes beside Frank, sometimes well behind him, sometimes up ahead, sometimes walking the bike up hills, all dependent upon his conditioning and teen urges.

There was Frank's dad, Frank Giannino Jr., nicknamed Sonny, commandeering the motor home. He was a retired male nurse, gruff, opinionated, and his son's biggest fan placed in charge of keeping Frank's body working well enough to travel 3,000 miles by foot.

There was Frank's step-mom Ja (pronounced Jay), her birth name Josephine Giacalone, lending unconditional support to Frank and her husband. She was the cook, the cleaner, the diary author and often the singular voice of reason.

And there was Bruce Goldberg, a journalist from back home. He was Frank's all-important public relations man and media liaison, maintaining contact with the main sponsor, United Way, and forging interviews for Frank along the way.

Four motorcycle policemen escorted the runners and John as they headed onto San Francisco's streets toward the Golden Gate Bridge. Frank soon gave John his first chore as they approached the San Francisco Bay. John must retrieve a plastic bottle of water from the Pacific Ocean. Frank planned to pour the water into the East River below the Brooklyn Bridge at the finish line as a symbolic gesture of the coast-to-coast run.

John performed his first main duty flawlessly and caught up to the runners on the walkway of the bridge. They were about a third of the way over the span, five miles from the starting line, when they came upon a commotion up ahead. A young couple approached the runners and warned them to discontinue the route.

"You can't run across here," the woman said. "There's a man down there threatening to commit suicide. They're waiting for his wife to come."

A man was situated on a narrow girder below the walkway. It looked like he was about to jump.

Frank had to make a snap decision. He could wait for the crowd to dissipate, which could take – who knows? – an hour or more. Not good. Frank was officially on the clock, every minute precious in his record-breaking quest. Darned if he was going to fall behind his pace only a few miles into the run.

Frank decided to continue the run on the opposite side of the bridge. He instructed his runners to join him in jumping the railing separating the walkway from six lanes of traffic.

"I can see the headlines now, 'Transcontinental run starts and ends in tragedy,'" Frank said.

"Or better yet," Goldberg offered, "'Runner run over avoiding suicide.'"

The runners dodged vehicles as they crossed the busy lanes of traffic toward the other side of the bridge. There was only one problem. John couldn't pull the same stunt on a bicycle. He needed to keep the mileage as accurately as possible for world-record recognition. So he disconnected the odometer helping measure the distance of the voyage.

Frank had gone to the American Automobile Association during his week in San Francisco to adopt the company's TripTik, a personalized map used to chart routes, once the sole method of navigating long distances. Like Frank's previous run, the idea was to stay off main highways because of traffic and, in many cases, local laws against navigating the thoroughfares by foot or bike. Frank and Goldberg spent a couple hours laying out the route, Bruce said, before they left for San Francisco. But Frank would soon learn that a folding map and directions are hardly foolproof no matter how many markings and arrows he had drawn up.

Worse, Goldberg claimed later, Frank arbitrarily changed most of the route after arriving in San Francisco while Goldberg remained in New York for a few additional days. Goldberg said the changes compromised all his work in setting up publicity opportunities with United Way offices along the original route.

Goldberg was, in his words "flabbergasted" that Frank pulled such a stunt. Such publicity was essential to both raising awareness and thus funds for the cause, and keeping Frank's mind fresh and positive knowing he had an audience.

Goldberg lamented the logistical screw-up and wondered how Frank could be so oblivious to the ramifications of changing the route. Goldberg obviously didn't know Frank very well. Frank was so focused on breaking the record that such a drastic measure as altering the route days before the start represented minor details by comparison.

One major detail was accurately measuring the run for Guinness-record acknowledgement. John's measurements were vital to true mileage readings. So he made his first snap judgment of the trip. He would mark the spot on the bridge and retrace his route, biking down the pedestrian path that led under the bridge and back to the walkway on the other side of the bridge. When he reached his marker on the opposite side, he would reconnect the odometer.

By now Frank had almost run the length of the bridge. But he was already stressed. His brother was nowhere in sight. His dad and step-mom in the motor home had to stay back in the crush of the suicide attempt. As Frank's anxiety heightened, he saw John furiously pumping his legs down the pedestrian path. Frank crossed the bridge and into a parking lot to meet the motor home in the planned reunion spot.

The honorary runners did their part. They returned to their normal lives while Frank continued to run for his life. A biker passed and noticed Frank's AAU (Amateur Athletic Union) T-shirt with his name across the front. The biker had seen Frank on a morning TV show.

"Yeah, that's me," Frank said.

"Hey man, why are you doing it?" the biker asked.

Frank laughed.

"Did you hear about the man on the bridge?" the biker continued.

"No," Frank said, "what happened to him?"

"His wife got there and he looked up at her and jumped."

No way. Frank couldn't believe the man actually had jumped. He had gone through with his threat and tragically completed his mission. Or maybe he had begun the day seeking attention and come to a snap decision, choosing death over life in an eye blink. Could life be that tenuous? That brittle? Could a man make the ultimate sacrifice for the singular purpose of gaining attention?

What exactly made him take the final plunge? Frank couldn't wrap his arms around it, not then, nor would he try.

"Yeah," the biker said, detailing the jumper doing a Hail Mary prayer before flying off the bridge.

Frank shared the information when he met up with his support team.

"Oh," Frank's dad said evenly.

"That's a shame," Ja said. "How unfair to his wife."

Frank's dad processed the news for a moment. Well, he said finally, "We are not going to let this jinx the run."

2

The First Cross-Country Run

The book all but reached out and grabbed Frank Giannino by the throat inside Bill Rodgers' running store in Boston. It was "My Run Across the United States," Don Shepherd's story of running from Los Angeles to New York in 1964 at age forty-eight.

Shepherd was the eighty-sixth person to complete a transcontinental run, performing the task in a tidy 73.35 days, an average of 43.7 miles a day. His was, according to usacrossers.com, John Wallace III's Web site listing transcontinental runs, the twenty-third fastest per-day tally in history.

Frank and a couple buddies were in town to run the 1978 Boston Marathon. He furiously flipped through the pages while his mind moved just as swiftly. Wow, Frank wondered! How cool would it be to do something like that? What better way to separate from the pack, to have that many eyes upon him, to be cheered by the masses? His friend Billy Glatz connected with the run just as fervently, or so it seemed.

"Can you imagine?" Billy said.

Frank and Billy had known each other for just a short time. They were both Eagle Scouts and running bums sharing a basement apartment by the mountains a half-dozen miles outside of New Paltz, New York. They had an affinity for partying and long-distance running and not much else. At that very moment, though, they shared something deep and powerful. They shared a dream. Frank was just shy of his twenty-sixth birthday and trying to decide what to do with his life. Why not figure it out from the road?

"There were my insecurities, his insecurities," Frank said. "He was a hippie right out of the book. People gravitated toward Billy in the community. He was inspiring as far as ideas. He had great ideas, from workouts to travel. I always felt second to Billy as far as his like-ability."

They shelved the idea until Christmas day eight months later, when Frank and Billy set out for a long early morning run before celebrating the holiday with family. The course was an adventurous fifteen-mile point-to-point mountaintop run on the famed Shawangunk Mountains. They ran from the Awosting Lake parking lot past Lake Maratanza and finished up at Cragsmoor Church, known as "The Stone Church" for its structure built from the mountain's stone more than one hundred years earlier.

"Billy," Frank said along the way, "let's do that run we talked about a while back. Remember last April, when we were in Boston for the marathon and stopped at Bill Rodgers' running store in Cleveland Circle? Remember, we agreed we would do that some day?"

"OK Frank,"Billy said finally. "You get the sponsor and some help and you got yourself a partner."

Frank seemed to need the run more than Billy, at twenty-six years younger. Billy was just as content enjoying the peaceful presence of running the Utopian hills and trails of the Hudson Valley, especially internationally known Minnewaska State Park just down the road from his running store.

He had come to Ulster County, ninety minutes up the Thruway from New York City, from his Harrison, Westchester County home to attend the State University of New York at New Paltz. Billy recently had dropped out of college to start his store, "Catch Us If You Can Running Center," with another mutual friend, Bob Bright, in New Paltz.

Glatz was smart (a biology major) and kind-hearted. But he was extremely complex, Frank said, an eccentric loner, shy,

11

introverted, even secretive. Billy kept a lot inside. Even his closest friends rarely knew Billy's innermost thoughts. Ask him his interests and he would turn coy before mentioning camping, hiking and skiing.

Frank helped out at the running store each day. But he was pretty much the polar opposite of Billy. Frank was outgoing and extroverted. He loved the sense of victory and camaraderie associated with running, but also the attention afforded those who produced extraordinary achievements. Frank was the proverbial open book, talking your ears off, advertising his thoughts and goals even while struggling to decipher them himself.

There was a sense of mystery to Frank as well. Frank had cleared his running schedule by quitting a part-time job as recreation director at a nearby organization for people with disabilities. Friends often wondered how much of Frank's openness and gift for gab were genuine or sprinkled with a natural or subconscious sales pitch used to propel his spirit like blades lifting a helicopter.

Billy was a hippie straight from the Woodstock Era. Frank had hippie tendencies – his VW van, his love for travel and adventure and waving a thumb for rides–but was a conservative at heart and would remain that way his whole life.

Frank naturally wanted to run across America in grand fashion – alerting the news media, using a support vehicle, getting sponsors. Billy wanted to run it with backpacks and as little fanfare as possible.

Frank wanted to run it for charity; Billy had no interest in dealing with sponsors. Frank wanted the world watching; Billy wanted to see the world.

"One of the worst things about running across America is not being recognized," Frank would say. "You are out there putting forth the effort and doing it for a cause. I think it's real important to be recognized. My whole thing was the adventure. I thought it would be kind of fun to see if I could do it. I liked that it embraced who I was as a human being."

Frank was searching for closure. He had run too many races to count. But the finish line eluded him. His life was an exercise in unfinished business, whether ceasing to participate in the Boy Scouts after receiving his Eagle award or quitting the short-lived garage band or his inability to win big races throughout school. Even the relationship with his mom was cloudy. Crossing the country on foot would overshadow, maybe eliminate, that exhausting feeling, and fear, of failure.

Frank was never more determined to silence the naysayers. But he needed to silence his deep insecurities just as ferociously. He needed to do something big. He needed to finish something.

The other runner in the trio, Bright, passed on the idea. He simply had no desire to do it. "It's about how long you can go before you die," Bright said years later. "But (Frank) knew he could do it. You could see it in his eyes."

At least Frank looked and sounded like he could do it. "The more people who doubted my ability to do it," he said, "the more I was inspired. I've always hoped for the best and planned for the worst. That was my slogan in life. It was all so outrageous. We knew nothing about support or survival. We didn't know the culture of people who did it. We didn't know about running, walking, pacing. We were thinking (of trying to maintain) forty miles a day. When we left, we decided on fifty miles a day. I had convinced a lot of people that I just knew I could do it – even myself.

"But I was scared to death."

Frank and Billy plotted their run from Los Angeles to New York. Frank finally got Billy to ditch the backpack idea on account of them being broke. They needed sponsors. They took in $1,200 for the run by selling vintage albums and stereo systems at a local flea market. But they needed more cash.

Frank used his powers of persuasion to get a local newspaper, *The Daily Freeman,* of Kingston, New York, to provide coverage of the run from start to finish. The paper put a map of the run above its banner on the front page, unprecedented ink for a local runner. The Freeman donated $500 and set up a pledge campaign – $2 a mile – to help bankroll the run and benefit Ulster County United Way. Donors paying for at least five miles would get a signed postcard by one of the runners along the route. Camper's Barn of Kingston donated the motor home. Billy was unhappy with the approach, but he handled it with typical silence.

Who would head the support team? That was easy. There was only one volunteer.

Becky Wright, 23, was a SUNY New Paltz student working as a high school substitute teacher and assistant girls track coach at hers and Frank's alma mater, Valley Central High School, 90 minutes north of New York City. She had run on the boys' team in high school because there was no girls' team.

Becky had barely known Frank other than watching him from afar in high school. She was an eighth-grader, he a senior, but her brother Mike – one of four siblings, including three brothers – was friends with Frank. Mike would come home talking about Frank's long-distance exploits, and Becky certainly was impressed with Frank in both high school and as he progressed into a high-level local road racer.

"At the time he was the epitome of the long-distance cross country runner," she said. "He was our local Frank Shorter."

Becky hung around Billy's store. She was introspective with a flair for writing poetry. She shared Frank's sense of adventure and love of nature and impulsiveness. While Mike referred to their home on Borden Road as Boredom Road, Becky embraced the peacefulness, the fresh air and settling scents of the woods.

"I loved hanging out in the woods," she said. "I was a country girl."

Becky and Frank had a lot in common without yet knowing it. Plus she lacked major commitments at the time. It was the perfect period in her life to take such a leap. She had no boyfriend. Her parents had moved to Florida and Becky needed some form of change in her life. She found the idea "really cool" and figured she might never get the opportunity to see a good chunk of the country in such detail.

Becky Wright was, by chance, the perfect person to crew for Frank.

Plus, well, she was the only candidate.

"I thought it was unbelievably unique and different," she said. "He just said, 'You want to do it?'"

"You really want me to do this?" she replied.

Becky would drive the camper and help organize the public relations efforts and incoming donations. She would massage his feet, wash his clothes, run errands – "a little housewife on wheels" was her self-description – and become Frank's non-judgmental guiding force toward the finish line.

The runners began to train seriously. But Frank and Billy were marathoners. They were comfortable with the 26.2-mile distance. They weren't ultra-marathoners, that special marathon-plus breed racing 100 milers like others chose 5Ks. Frank's long-distance resume pretty much began and ended with a credible 2:39:34 clocking in the 1975 Maryland Marathon, good for twenty-eighth overall.

Their first major training run was a 40-miler at an 8:30 per-mile clip. They decided on a three-day, 100-mile run to Albany to show prospective sponsors, and themselves, that they could run the longer distances necessary to complete the task. Frank came up with an idea to finish the run at the capitol building, where he would visit Governor. Hugh Carey to get his endorsement. They ran the twenty-nine miles from Middletown to New Paltz through a torrential downpour on the first day. They got lost running through Kingston on day two, all the while running a suicidal seven-eight-per-mile pace.

Frank's legs were killing him. He put supports under both heels to ease the strain on his Achilles' tendons. Billy was hurting as well. They reached Albany on the third day. But when Frank sought a meeting with Governor Carey, he was told that popping in on the governor hardly ranked as the preferred method of securing face time. Frank was embarrassed. How could he possibly think he could see the governor without an appointment?

Billy was bitter. "What was it all for?" he said. "Nobody even knows we made this damn run. It was all a waste, man. A total waste."

"No it wasn't," Frank told him. "We proved we can do it."

Frank met a podiatrist in Santa Monica, Dr. Robert Mohr, a week before the run. Even that meeting was hardly the product of planning. They had come upon Dr. Mohr's office on a training run on Sunset Boulevard near the starting line and paid a visit.

The podiatrist outfitted Frank and Billy with custom orthotics, the first time Frank had ever worn professional inserts. They were made of natural cork and neoprene.

Their diet was quite sophisticated. They would try to maintain 7,000 calories daily with an emphasis on carbohydrates and protein shakes. A local doctor told *The Freeman* that running for charity would help motivate Frank and Billy, calling it, "a radical concept."

On March 1, 1979, with a one-person support team using TripTiks, a twenty-foot Coachman motor home with a sign in front reading, "Run Across America," Frank Giannino and Billy Glatz began their 2,876-mile run from Los Angeles to New York. A buddy Frank had met in the Army, Mike Leming, joined them for the first few days of the trip.

Problems began immediately. Frank and Billy had to change their route at the last minute after being barred by police authorities from running on interstate highways in California and Arizona. The team left Malibu Beach amid a downpour with almost no sleep the previous night as partiers celebrated loudly nearby.

Within two hours of their start, Frank and Billy got lost. They went four miles past the planned meeting spot with Becky and Mike, near Sunset Drive and Sepulveda Boulevard, and wound up running some fifty miles, sans support, while trying to find the crew. With pay phones the only means of communication, Becky was forced to call the Los Angeles police, who launched a search and distributed pictures that a UPI photographer had taken of the pair at the start that morning. Hungry and with little money, Frank and Billy stopped in diners and were given muffins and sandwiches to ease their empty stomachs.

They eventually met up with the crew, but crisis turned to conflict as arguments ensued between Mike and Becky, and then between Billy and Becky, and then between Becky and Frank, over who was responsible for the situation. Mike decided to leave after the first day and Frank learned his first lesson of cross-country running: less delegating, more leading.

"I started taking control," he said.

There is one thing Frank had no control over, however: Billy

Glatz.

"The more organized the effort became," Frank said of Billy, "the more there were signs of him pulling away."

On Day Two, Glatz, who was fair-skinned with long blond hair, became an inviting target for sun poisoning by running through the Mojave Desert in a black T-shirt without having applied sunscreen. "He started falling off the pace the first fifteen minutes," Frank said. "I could see he was struggling. Whenever I slowed down, he said, 'Go ahead.' We had agreed that one person would not hold the other person back."

Frank, right, and Billy Glatz, 1979.

They distanced fifty miles that day and stayed in a motel room. But it was hardly a good night's sleep for Billy. He was overcome by sun poisoning. Lying on the floor of the hotel room, his entire body started to tremble as if he were enduring an epileptic seizure. He refused to go to the hospital, and at 6 a.m. the following morning over breakfast, Billy broke the news to Frank.

"I'm dropping out."

"It was like a divorce the moment the announcement was made," Frank said. "To me, it was out of the blue. In every way possible, I had to do this – for therapy, my life path, cleansing. I needed it; it had to happen. Billy didn't need it. He would say to me, 'You need it more than me.'"

Frank was disappointed and hurt. Deep down he thought Billy was searching for an out, that his decision to run in tormenting sun without protection was a calculated decision. But Frank also was relieved. Now he could focus solely on making it across the country.

Said Becky of Billy's departure, "All the tension left."

Billy hung with Frank and Becky for nine days as a handler to make sure Frank would be okay. When they reached Phoenix, Billy stuck out his thumb. A trucker stopped and Billy got the ride of his life. He was home within forty-eight hours of stepping into the truck.

Becky and Frank were in no hurry to share the news with a larger audience. They told the media on Day Eleven, with Frank informing a *Freeman* reporter that he would make it alone "come hell or high water.'"

"My confidence was never shaken," Frank said.

He found his groove running five-mile intervals ten times a day. Frank went fifteen miles before breakfast, twenty miles before lunch and thirteen to fifteen miles before devouring a large dinner at the end of the day. He started to consistently record fifty-mile days. Frank stopped every five miles for water and a candy bar.

"Cinnamon buns with icing; protein powder in liquids; he was just running on sugar," Becky said. "He'd take a big tub of Vaseline and smear it on his feet. The blisters on his feet were so big. They were really awful. It was very hard to see him go through that ... that human suffering. Sometimes I'd massage his feet and legs and he'd be in so much pain. He really suffered for a goal, but he was so driven. I couldn't believe how determined he was. He seemed to always believe he could do it, so I believed he could do it."

Becky wanted to tell Frank that it was okay if he quit. But she knew there was no place for such negativity. Not once did Frank talk about quitting.

"He always remained positive; at least he didn't let me hear (any negativity)," she said. "The best I could do was try to support him."

Wright also vouched for the authenticity of the run, an affirmation that would prove crucial in years ahead. "If we stop for the night and drive ahead, even two-tenths of a mile to a rest area to spend the night, he goes back the next morning to start where we stopped the night before," she told a newspaper.

Frank's mind was so strong that he not only ignored the pain but denied it entirely. The blisters Becky witnessed were minimized to a single blister, at least in Oklahoma, halfway home, when Frank told *The Oklahoma Journal*, "So far I've had only one blister on my feet. The key to the whole thing is to keep your mind on something else. It's really not so bad once you get the hang of it."

They listened to the Eagles and The Allman Brothers Band and other classic rock bands. Becky occasionally extended the speakers out of the camper so Frank could hear the music while running. Sometimes she ran a bit with him before heading back to the ride.

Frank described Becky as his "psychological coach" by helping him remain positive. "She was always upbeat and positive," he said. "I needed that kind of encouragement. She also took care of support details by herself. She was constantly there for more. I could not have asked for more from a support person."

"There were times when I really enjoyed it," Becky said, "and times when I thought, 'Can somebody rescue me?'

"We were washing stuff out in this little sink. It was a little sketchy at times. He had this scruffy beard; he really looked like Forrest Gump. We looked like hippies."

As the run dragged on, Becky started to miss her family and friends and apartment back home. She missed amenities such as a real shower and a real bed. At times she used the written word to sprout from her malaise, her poetry a healing agent stronger than any therapist. A poem she penned:

Branches coated with
a winter rainstorm clatter
in conversation.

Moss clings to the north
side of a tree playing hide
and seek with the sun.
Leaves fall on muddy
puddles and race ...
tiny boats pushed by Autumn breezes.
The poplar tips and
turns its leaves against the wind
an approaching storm.
After a spring rain
a spider web cries
a necklace of tears.
The sulphur moth quiet
and dancing, whispers into
the heart of a flame.

In Missouri, Frank talked about increasing to sixty-mile days and doing "four or five seventy-mile runs." His pace slowed near St. Louis because of a sore shin tendon in his left leg. Frank inserted a quarter-inch heel lift and soldiered on, slowing his nine- to ten-minute pace to ten- and eleven-minute miles. He endured a consistent onslaught of rain leading into St. Louis, with cars stopped along roads and a trailer park about to be washed away from flooding. Cars floated along roads and water reached doorways of homes. A doctor in St. Louis gave Frank another heel lift and surgical over-the-calf compression hoses to aid his recovery. Frank had a little less than one thousand miles to go. The injury healed in two weeks. It had to heal. Frank had no intention of quitting.

But he had a heck of a time running on worn-out shoes. Frank went through three pairs of running shoes faster than expected and couldn't get EEE-width shoes anywhere. Thankfully, a New Balance store in St. Louis donated three pairs.

Missouri also was memorable for representing those less accepting of Frank and Becky's journey. They were in a church parking lot when a guy chased them away, gun in hand.

In Indiana, he told a local newspaper that he was making the run for a number of reasons. He said he was trying to reach a goal he had set thirteen years earlier when he first started running. He said he was promoting volunteerism for United Way chapters across America. It all sounded good.

Frank got separated from Becky one more time, taking a wrong turn in Doylestown, Pennsylvania, 2,800 miles into the run, as he burned unnecessary miles before police again reunited the pair. Seven Bucks County police departments searched for more than two hours before finding an exhausted Giannino at a 7-Eleven store on Route 611 in Doylestown.

It's funny. Frank had all these deep-rooted reasons for doing the run, the deepest being that empty feeling of unfulfillment that had muddied his life. But the feelings were buried in his subconscious. More pressing was a whole other mound of rejection and failure, more recent and undoubtedly enlivening his childhood demons. As it turned out, Frank's first run across the country could be traced to his love for something other than adventure and the wilderness and open roads.

It could be traced to his love for another race, the female race, namely blondes, specifically a woman named Patty Whelan.

They had met through Bob Bright in the fall of '75 while students at SUNY New Paltz, a half-hour from Frank's home in Walden. Frank had gone to study math with plans to become a math teacher. He thrived with concrete mathematical concepts. But he couldn't grasp the theoretical elements of math.

He found something much more important to him at the time – love. On the second day of the semester, Frank and Bob were on a run when Bright introduced Frank to Patty, herself out for a run.

Frank was, in his words, "awestruck by her beauty." Patty was a former prom queen with a contagious smile, blue eyes and long blond hair.

"I never thought I would be with a woman like her," Frank said. "Every time I was to be with her, I would get butterflies with anticipation. Most of all, she was fun to be with. I was truly in love with her."

They talked about a future together. Patty, a second-year student at New Paltz, would get her degree in special education,

Frank in parks management. They would get married, have children and live a life of romance and happiness.

They transferred to Northern Arizona University in Flagstaff to finish their degrees, and they lived together at NAU. But Frank was immature. He busted on Patty without knowing the depth of his barbs until it was too late. She became friendly with a guy from San Diego while Frank spent long hours in the evening working at a local pizza parlor. One night he came home from work and she had moved out. The seventeen-month romance was over.

It shook Frank's outlook on women and his ability to forge serious relationships. He had a few flings at the school – "revenge sex," he called It – hurting his share of women along the way.

"I was completely devastated when she told me she was sleeping with another guy," he said. "I was so crushed. I remember that I couldn't breathe. Many of us know that feeling.

"Because I truly loved that girl. Once you can experience that, you can never duplicate that. As a result, your guard goes up."

Frank was almost as committed to girls and women as he was to running. Many of his childhood memories revolved around females, not just the clichéd first kiss and maiden turns at more deliberate advances, but deeper memories that he carried into adulthood. Some men dismiss young romances entirely while others wonder what-if, while still others cling to a feeling of regret over the one that got away.

Patty, more than anyone and perhaps more than anything, inadvertently sent Frank on his first run across the country. Frank felt a sense of confidence at being able to forge a relationship with such a smart and beautiful woman. Yet he also felt the pang of loneliness and failure. He needed to figure out things. He needed the healing powers of nature.

He needed to run.

"The one thing that gave me true relief," he said of the breakup, "was running."

On April 30, Frank's twenty-seventh birthday, he arrived at the finish line, the middle of the pedestrian footpath on the

Brooklyn Bridge. He had completed 2,876 miles in 60.25 days, an average of 48.07 miles a day. It was, at the time, the ninth fastest recorded crossing. Frank was the 103rd person to run across the United States, according to usacrossers.com.

Blue and white squad cars with blaring sirens accompanied Frank as he carried a United Way banner across the bridge and continued onto City Hall for the finish ceremony. The media turnout was modest. In fact, according to Kingston newspaper, the only New York media outlets were Channel 11 News and a radio station.

"Anybody want to run to Los Angeles?" Frank said as family and friends surrounded him at the foot of the steps to City Hall.

"You can do anything if you have enough desire," he told Deputy Mayor Herman Badillo, himself a marathoner, at City Hall.

Joe Kleinerman, founder of the New York Road Runners Club, presented Frank with a gold medallion. Kleinerman said Frank's effort on behalf of charity had won him the club's support, according to an account in *The Freeman*.

Frank left New York the next morning for a casual two-day, sixty-mile run that consisted of camping out in Harriman State Park in southern Orange County and running from nearby Tuxedo to Kingston's Dietz Stadium for another ceremony, with a stopover in his hometown of Walden to celebrate Frank Giannino Day.

People lined Broadway Street in Kingston to create a parade-like atmosphere, three and four rows deep in some spots, an estimated ten thousand folks in all, as Frank led the way. About seventy-five locals joined Frank heading into Dietz Stadium, its plush track-rimmed football home of the Kingston High Tigers. A brass band played and kids requested Frank's autograph. He mentioned the idea of writing a book about the experience. Kingston Mayor Francis R. Koenig presented Frank with a key to the city. Donations to United Way on Frank's behalf totaled $11,700 – mostly mail-in donations – and about $4,000 went to the organization after expenses.

"The thing I remember most was feeling the trust and friendship that Becky had provided for two months," Frank said later. "She was really loyal."

Yet by the time Frank had crossed the official finish line, he already was feeling a familiar sense of unfulfillment.

"I knew when I finished the first run that I had not given it my all," he said. "We were finishing fifty-mile runs with time left in the day."

He knew he could go faster.

He knew he had to do it again.

The first run was about completing a monumental task while trying to decipher the pain of shattered love. The second run was going to be about setting a world record.

By the time Frank set out on his second run across the United States sixteen months later, one hundred and six runners had succeeded in going at least twenty-eight hundred miles across different parts of the country. The hundred and sixth runner to do it earlier in the year was a man named Stan Cottrell, who ran from New York City to San Francisco in 48.08 days. Cottrell averaged 64.56 miles a day, the measurement Guinness was using for its record. Cottrell held the world record.

Frank wanted Cottrell's record. In fact, Frank felt like he *needed* the record.

3

Where's Modupe?

Frank and Billy Glatz were on a sixteen-mile training run, navigating Route 299 toward the Undercliff/Overcliff section of the Shawangunk Mountains, as the summer of 1979 approached. It was a month since Frank had turned his first cross-America run into a solo adventure after Billy, suffering from extreme sun poisoning, quit days from the start.

Billy's emotions suddenly engulfed Frank with the force of a fire extinguisher. Billy was fighting mad at Frank for ignoring Billy's desires leading to the run across America, for being the sole spokesman, for not deferring questions to Billy. Glatz, after all, was a knowledgeable runner sharp enough to make a buck selling running shoes in high school and co-owning a running store, one of the first of its kind in the Hudson Valley.

They began arguing and Frank never saw what happened next. Billy spit in Frank's face.

"I was so humiliated the rest of the run," Frank said. "I think quitting, for him, set a path for the rest of his life."

It was the last time they ever ran together. Billy never apologized, Frank said, and later left New Paltz to start a running store in Plattsburgh, New York, located in the North Country an hour outside of Montreal. Billy would return to the Hudson Valley in 1984 to open a new running store in New Paltz. Frank met up with Billy again in 1987 when Billy walked into Frank's own running store to sell him a line of running clothing. Frank said that Billy told him to pay up "whenever" to give Frank time to move the items. A week later, Billy unexpectedly showed up at Frank's home needing the $600 for the order "in cash" right then and there. Frank paid Billy the cash, and that was it. They never saw each other again.

Frank felt bad for the relationship gone sour. He wondered if he should have done things differently, perhaps allowed Billy to have a greater voice in planning the run. Such second-guessing was typical of Frank. But Frank knew that Billy's idea to backpack across the country wasn't going to work. They needed sponsorship. They needed a support team, even if it was a support team of one, Becky Wright. They needed a plan, for crying out loud.

Frank felt like a celebrity around New Paltz after his transcontinental run. Folks cornered him on the street, in bars, wanting to talk about the run. He went to work at the Mohonk Mountain House, a resort hotel on the Shawangunk Ridge in the town of New Paltz. Frank got free room and board. A limousine occasionally pulled up to take him to United Way fund raisers as the guest speaker.

"I did a little bit of everything," he said.

Frank started thinking about another run across the country. But his life reflected his training runs on the rolling hills of the Hudson Valley – up and down, down and up – tragedy and failure usually a stride or two from euphoria and accomplishment.

In the summer of '79, Frank was a water-safety instructor for the New Paltz summer recreation program at New Paltz High School. He and fellow employees would take more than two hundred kids in the program on field trips to various locations in the Catskill Mountains. This summer's trip involved a swim day under the promising sunshine at Tillson Lake, part of the Minnewaska State Park Preserve just outside New Paltz.

Each worker was responsible for eight to ten kids ages six through twelve. Each kid made up a two-swimmer "buddy team" to help ensure safety in the water. As a safeguard, Frank initiated "buddy checks" every fifteen minutes, in which the kids left the

26

water for head counts. They returned to the water after the buddy check.

They were enjoying the water one ninety-degree day when Frank suddenly heard an eerie call from a young swimmer.

"Where's Modupe?"

Modupe Clarke was an eight-year-old girl from Trinidad whose parents had moved to New Paltz weeks earlier. She was part of the only three-person buddy system in the three-foot deep water.

"We don't know where she went," a young girl said.

The kids were sent out of the water and twenty-five employees, in two rows, formed a human chain in a search-and-rescue mission. *Where's Modupe?* They checked one side of their play area. Nothing. Counselors prayed Modupe would turn up on land. Maybe she had come out of the lake to take a walk. Maybe she had slipped away without anybody noticing. Could be anything.

The counselors split into teams of people diving into the water to check the bottom. They again formed a human chain to check the other side of the play area. No Modupe.

Suddenly a teen counselor wading through the water next to Frank bumped into something. It was Modupe Clarke, the little girl from Trinidad. Her body was tangled in lake weed amid the murky waters.

Frank grabbed a blanket from a family on the beach and, along with a lifeguard, performed CPR on Modupe. It was too late. Little Modupe Clarke was dead.

Frank figured she was under water for twenty minutes.

"It was a failure," Frank said. "I wasn't able to save that girl. I was responsible for her life."

Frank was crushed. He informed the parents as they arrived to pick up their children. Later, Modupe's dad visited Frank's store and wound up consoling Frank.

"She was beautiful," Frank said. "To this day, it haunts me."

Frank's feelings of helplessness and insecurity came charging back. He tried running in a local Summer Series race he had planned to do the next day. Frank stopped before the finish line, sobbing. He had just finished running across the United States, just conquered an enormous obstacle that was supposed to bring comfort and clarity. Yet Frank couldn't prevent an eight-year-old girl from drowning in a lake crowded with swimmers.

He tried to focus his thoughts on planning the second run. Frank wanted to do this one the right way, with a full support team and major sponsors. But despite a successful transcontinental finish under his belt, he was having trouble securing any type of sponsorship.

Frank lacked name recognition. He wasn't a world-class runner like Frank Shorter or Bill Rodgers. And these journey runs were unappealing to many prospective sponsors.

One company after another rejected Frank's sales pitch. And to Frank, something of a local hero only, that amounted to rejecting him.

But Frank figured he would make at least one major improvement on his second run. He would form a sound support team. It was no knock on Becky Wright. She did a marvelous job steering Frank's first run. But there were far too many duties for one person to handle adeptly. Frank was trying to formulate the details of his team when his dad broached the topic at dinner one night.

Why not have the family – Dad and Ja and John – make up the team?

"That would be great, Dad," Frank said, "but there's a lot of pressure on the support crew. It's not easy."

"I know, but think about it Frank," his dad said, "Who else can you really count on when things get tough except your family?"

Frank's father had just retired after thirty years as a corrections facility nurse. And come to think of it, he had told his son at the finish line of Frank's first run that Dad would head the support team for the second adventure. Frank's father felt obligated to insulate his son from the many potential pitfalls of a three thousand-mile run.

Frank was skeptical. He appreciated the loyalty and commitment of loved ones. But he wondered if the crew could endure his heightened expectations of them, expectations he knew would rise in direct correlation to Frank's own pain and suffering along the route.

Frank finally saw merit in the plan. There was no substitute for sharing the adventure with family. And like Dad said, if you can't trust family, who could you trust?

Dad would seem to be an ideal crew leader steering the motor home and soothing his son's broken-down body. Ja would be a calming influence without motive or agenda, just the desire to see her stepson become the fastest person to run across the United States. Her tasty meals would be of great benefit as well.

"Nobody who ran across the country had the cooking I had," Frank said.

And John? John would be a Godsend riding beside his big brother every step of the way. The family navigated one potential obstacle by receiving Board of Education approval for him to miss the first seven weeks of school. They worked out an arrangement that included accompanying John with books and sending him work to complete along the route.

John had a greater concern. He had no training on a bicycle other than, as he put it, riding one growing up. He had no long-distance driving experience or, of course, any miles hard by tractor trailers or against the screams of Mother Nature or long stretches up and down hills.

Frank wasn't the only adventurous family member. John climbed aboard.

John and Frank picked up the bike two weeks before leaving. John figured they would grab something workable, not too fancy, perhaps in the $200 range. The bike would reflect his no-frills nature. John was stunned when the family decided on a pricey Fuji mountain bike. "I just wanted something comfortable," he said.

The seat was padded and John had two pairs of padded biker shorts. He started off with a boom box, the bulky 1970s mini-stereo that fit cassette tapes, strapped to the back and a pouch for bare necessities –toilet paper, water and fresh fruit. John would put the stereo in the motor home after about a week, tired of changing batteries and cassette tapes. But no matter what he lugged or how smooth the ride, there was no bike on the market comfortable enough to withstand the torturous pain of pedaling three thousand miles.

So it was a go. Frank's dad, Ja and John would make up Frank's support team. Of course, they would bring along Brindle, Sonny and Ja's happy-go-lucky fifteen-year-old dachshund/poodle mix. Brindle already had played a special role in the Giannino household, renewing Ja's love of dogs after she had been bitten by one early in her life.

Frank's support team was just about set. But he was less than two months from the start of the run and still without sponsorship. Frank was starting to give up on getting sponsorship. He decided he was going to bankroll the run with modest savings and credit cards when an angel fell from the sky. His name was Bud Weiner, a local track and field official who at one time owned several shoe stores in Rockland County, each with a different niche within the shoe industry.

Frank had gone to high school with two of Weiner's sons, Michael and Jeff. Bud Weiner had become a sales representative for Intermark Shoe Company, a division of International Seaway Trading Corporation. The company was trying to promote a brand of running shoes called AAU Shoes. (In fact Weiner had another claim to fame, according to Frank. He had called a foul on a young long jumper named Carl Lewis during the 1982 National Sports Festival in Indianapolis in what would have been the world's first thirty-foot jump.)

Weiner called Frank after seeing a story in a local newspaper on the upcoming run. Weiner set up a meeting between Frank and Intermark at the New York Coliseum on Columbus Circle, near the finish line of the New York City Marathon. Frank not only secured sponsorship from Intermark, based in Ohio, that day at the coliseum. He got to meet Stan Cottrell, who had just finished his record-breaking run and was said to be making big money in sales.

They didn't talk much at the show. But Frank saw Cottrell as the polar opposite of himself, a keenly organized, polished businessman. Frank saw something more vividly. He saw the huge map of Cottrell's world record-setting cross country run displayed at the exhibit.

Later in the day, Frank, Stan and Dave McGillivray, who would later direct that little New England race called the Boston Marathon, got together. All three had run across America. "We were very supportive of each other," Frank said. "We were comparing notes. There was no ego."

As part of Frank's two-year contract, according to Frank, Intermark agreed to pay him for expenses incurred during the run and a $10,000 sum paid at the conclusion of the run. Intermark also would supply the motor home needed as the support vehicle. In return, Frank would endorse AAU Shoes during the year following the run, as well as help develop and promote the company's new line of AAU running shoes.

Frank during a training run for the Boston Marathon in March 1980 on Springtown Road, New Paltz, New York.

The start of the run was just more than a month away when Frank crossed paths with a sports writer from the Kingston newspaper named Bruce Goldberg. They knew each other casually from the local running scene. Goldberg asked if Frank could use a PR guy.

"Sure," Frank said without hesitation, not thinking to run it past his family. "I need a PR guy!"

There were problems from the start. Ja and Frank's dad drove to Canton to pick up the motor home and take it to San Francisco to meet Frank, John and Bruce, all of whom had flown in eight days before the start. It was the only motor home available for the Gianninos, and for good reason. The vehicle wasn't exactly a limo on wheels. It was five years old and had been driven extensively. The interior water pump broke on their first day out of Canton. Water flooded the entire floor and soaked many of their belongings. The water tank had a crack in it, minimizing water flow to a single quick shower. The refrigerator door latch broke and items fell onto the floor.

Frank had his own issues in the Bay Area. A week before the start, he met Chris Smith and Richard Bogdan, instructors in the biomechanics department at California College of Podiatric Medicine. They introduced Frank to plastic orthotics, a running tool that would help define his business model years later.

Smith and Bogdan made two sets of orthotics and ran tests on Frank. They learned that Frank's running mechanics presented many challenges. Frank was born with a lateral curvature in both feet. For the first six months of his life, Frank's tiny body was in his cast to deal with the condition. Frank's father reminded him that had he not been in the cast, things might have been different. He has a rigid foot with low arches and Morton's Foot, a condition in which the second toe is longer than the big toe. Also known as Morton's Toe, it can cause all kinds of pain and discomfort and lead to more complicated foot problems. Frank had developed massive shin splints in high school as a result of his running shoes aggravating the condition.

The two best ways to combat Morton's Foot issues are orthotics and proper shoes. Smith and Bogdan took care of the orthotics. Finding the best running shoe was significantly more complicated given Frank's alliance with AAU Shoes. Frank wasn't nuts about the shoes, but he had only two choices. He needed to make the shoes as comfortable and workable as possible, or find another sponsor. With the run just days away, option two was eliminated.

Frank's footwear quickly became dwarfed by an alarming pronouncement from Smith and Bogdan. They examined Frank's running body thoroughly, noting the leg-length discrepancy caused by a ski accident, and various biomechanical issues. Standing with arms extended, Frank resisted when they pushed down on his left arm, but he offered no resistance when they pushed down on his right arm. Frank had been able to push through the right-side weakness during shorter races, sometimes barely swinging his right arm in latter portions of events. But he was about to attempt another three thousand-mile run. Finally, Smith and Bogdan shared with Frank their conclusion:

"You are not going to finish this thing."

It could have been the final dart in Frank's hopes of setting the transcontinental record. He already had endured massive indifference from prospective sponsors. He had gone through a shaky cross-country experience with his friend bowing out. Now Frank was being told by highly qualified specialists to quit while he was ahead.

Frank wasn't interested in taking the advice of Smith and Bogdan. He had a great deal of respect for them, knew their orthotics were well ahead of the times. But Frank was too focused to be denied by anything or anybody. He chalked up his leg issues as another challenge to be conquered.

"I'm committed and I'm going to do it," he told Smith and Bogdan. "What can you do to help ensure my goal?"

They gave him orthotics. Frank used the inserts and running tips he had stored away from his first trans-con adventure. Departure was twenty-four hours away.

Frank's aunt threw a going-away party for the crew at her home in Oakland. Many Gianninos were in attendance, including sisters Marijean and Barbara with their husbands, Jim and Lee. Frank's support staff and The World of People crew, a documentary company doing a story on the run, were on hand. It was a memorable occasion with cake-throwing and other mischief, guitar playing and singing by Bruce and Frank.

Still, Frank felt a bit funny about Bruce. Frank couldn't decipher his feelings. Something just felt strange to him. Frank said a red flag might have been Goldberg's family throwing a similar bash for Bruce back in New York before he left to join the run team in California. Frank felt odd about the party being thrown for Goldberg, who had decided to leave his newspaper job, as if he were the one running three thousand miles.

Goldberg, however, said his family never threw him a going-away party. "Don't know how Frank came up with that one," Goldberg said later.

"I had trepidation about why he was there and a basic discomfort about him being there," Frank said. "I worried about him meshing. He was not family. I never stated my concerns to anyone else."

The next morning, everyone at the party met at the steps of San Francisco City Hall. The pain of Run II wasn't going to be confined to his body. Frank's new-and-improved support team would start to break down long before he did.

4

Six Million Footsteps

Frank's dad, Frank Giannino Jr., was born in 1922 in Auburn, New York, a tiny Finger Lakes region town that, according to its Web site, was known best for having a correctional facility. Not long ago, Forbes Magazine ranked Auburn the eighteenth best small city in the nation to raise a family, and Number One in the Northeast.

The thirty thousand-population city, located thirty-five miles west of Syracuse and one hundred twenty miles east of Buffalo, has a rich cultural and arts history. National landmarks include the Harriet Tubman Home and the William Seward House. And for sports fans, the city probably is best known for hosting the Auburn Doubledays, a minor league baseball team since 1958 named after Civil War general Abner Doubleday, who grew up in Auburn and was mythically credited with inventing baseball. (Doubleday was a cadet in the United States Military Academy at West Point the year he supposedly invented the game.)

Frank Jr. grew up amid the heightened popularity of entertainer Al Jolson. Younger Frank suspects Dad's nickname – Sonny – derived from Jolson's hit single "Sonny Boy," which topped the charts for twelve weeks and sold a million copies, though Sonny was a common moniker among Italian patriarchs in the mid-twentieth century. Folks wrestled with correctly pronouncing Giannino (Gee-a-knee-no), so Frank Jr. was known as Sonny Gino, at least by family members and close friends.

There was the time Sonny decked a prison guard at Walkill Correctional Facility for calling him Sonny in a light-hearted manner. It showed Sonny's potentially volatile temper, something his children would rarely witness but always remembered.

Sonny was stationed in England during World War II when he met a woman. They shared a love for Lindy dancing and grew close, and by family accounts planned to marry. That all changed one day when Sonny got a call back home from a woman named Marion (Hitchens) Bryant. She had news for Sonny Gino. Her sister Ruth, Sonny's old girlfriend from Auburn, was pregnant.

Raised a Catholic, Sonny felt there was only one thing to do. It was the admirable thing. It was the right thing. He came home and married Ruth Hitchens.

They lived in Auburn while Frank Jr. finished his stint in the Army. He had been a machinist by trade in Auburn, working for a company called International Harvester that made machinery for farmland worldwide. But Sonny had become a medic in the Army after entrance tests revealed his aptitude for medicine. Upon his release, Sonny used his G.I. Bill for schooling.

On May 10, 1946, Ruth gave birth to a girl. They named her Marijean. Barbara arrived a year later, and Ruth and Sonny raised the girls in Auburn until 1951. Ruth wanted her husband to better himself by pursuing medicine via the G.I. bill, so they moved into a small apartment in the Rockland County village of Nyack, twenty miles north of Manhattan. They relocated to nearby Camp Shanks, a two thousand-acre area in Rockland that housed about fifty thousand World War II troops. On April 30, 1952, Frank Giannino III was born at Nyack Hospital.

Nancy was born in December 1955 and finally John, the baby, entered the world on New Year's Day 1963, almost 18 years after Marijean.

Five Giannino kids. Three girls. Two boys.

And one adventurous soul who was clearly out of the ordinary.

***

Frank knew he had better make major modifications from the first run. He had to improve drastically from his cross-America debut to beat Stan Cottrell's record pace of 64½ miles per day. Frank needed to add 16½ miles a day from his 48.07-mile tally the previous year.

It would seem to be virtually impossible. Frank viewed it as perfectly attainable. He had spent most of his twenty-eight years adjusting and modifying his quirky personality to fit in with the surroundings. Now it was time for him to adjust and modify his greatest love: running.

Frank rethought everything from the previous run. He decided first to change his stride to a shuffle. It would be lighter on his feet and exert less overall energy. Whereas each stride in his first run distanced 3½ feet, he would take more comfortable 2½-foot strides this time. Bruce Tulloh wrote a book called "Four Million Footsteps" about his run from Los Angeles to New York in 1969. Frank estimated that his run would require six million footsteps.

A shorter stride would help produce energy-saving ten- to fourteen-minute miles. Frank figured to incorporate five-minute walks sandwiched around 2.5-mile runs as another method to increase daily mileage and reduce weariness. It was a major change from running every step of five-mile clips in his first run.

Frank decided on longer intervals as well. He would take one-hour breaks every twenty-five miles – to eat, hydrate and study road maps as he planned the course while calculating his pace against the record.

"Some mornings I ran while asleep," he swore. "It doesn't matter if you walk or run – you just keep moving."

He would rise at three a.m. and take his first steps at four. Between regular meals, he would meet up with the motor home to grab food and drinks on the go from his father outside the driver's side window. Diluted orange juice with a dose of sugar was a popular choice to give him a much-needed jolt. Frank would grab Ja's homemade muffins from his dad for a carbohydrate boost. The idea was to keep moving, keep churning – one step at a time across the United States. Frank's only delay might be a two- or three-second stop at the Giannino snack stand before resuming running or walking.

"The key was to get as many daylight hours as we could," Frank said. "I would do the first three miles without (fully) waking up. The horizon motivated me every day. I was always looking for the first peek of daylight."

Yet no matter what method he chose, there would be no avoiding one constant theme: There was going to be a lot of pain – consistent pain, daily pain, shooting pain, extreme pain – sometimes constant pain. Frank knew from the first run that surviving and thriving was all about forcing his mind to listen to screeching declarations from his body.

Frank started with twenty pairs of AAU Shoes. Twenty more pairs would be waiting in Salt Lake City, assuming the originals wore out. But Frank would realize, by the second half of the run, that he got his best shoe comfort rotating six pairs every two days and changing shoes three times daily.

The plan was to reach Fort Collins, Colorado – roughly twelve hundred miles – on a sixty-mile per-day pace and then ramp it up to a record-breaking rate. But the challenges began on Day One. And like many challenges during the run, they involved the support team as much as they did the runner.

The first hurdle arrived with the disruption on the Golden Gate Bridge. My gosh, for all of the planning – at least considerably more planning than for Frank's maiden voyage – there was no compensation for a guy jumping off a bridge.

Then there was overnight parking. His family quickly realized that they couldn't just park the motor home on the side of the highway and call it a night. It was a bit of an eye sore, not to mention an obstruction that tended to be noticed by local authorities. The Gianninos had to find a campground or a relatively serene area to stop overnight, and finding campgrounds without detailed information on maps became a constant chore. Such was another burden of relying on TripTik, AAA's trip-planning feature perhaps best described in the new millennium as the anti-GPS.

John began experiencing discomfort almost immediately. Sometimes the pain was in his lower back. But the worst discomfort found its way up the inside of his thighs. John already was having a heck of a time getting used to being on his bicycle seat for extended periods of time. And he hated the Spandex bike shorts.

"God, Frank, why the hell do I have to wear these shorts?" he asked early on while battling thirty-mile-per-hour winds. "They're driving me crazy. You should try wearing pants with a leather crotch."

"Come on Turk," Frank said, employing the nickname he had just given John. It was usually an affectionate moniker, short for "Turkey," but often attached to "Fucking," as in, "Fucking Turkey." Thankfully, John was a great sport. "It's not leather," Frank told Turk. "It's chamois. You'll be glad you have them on before this run is over. You'll get used to it."

They broke for lunch at twenty miles. After eating, they encountered their first visitor, a very large bearded man who approached carrying a huge backpack. He was parched and sun beaten and dirty, and Frank would have been his usual engaging self under normal circumstances.

But these were far from normal circumstances. Frank was eager to start the post-lunch portion of his run. There was no time for chit-chat, no matter how odd the sight of a very large bearded man walking alone toward San Francisco, California.

"Hello, how are you," Frank said.

"Howdy," the man replied.

John picked up the conversation from there. "What are you doing out here?" he asked.

"Just walking across the country."

The man said he was finishing his own cross-country trek. He had begun from the East Coast and bore an odor that suggested he was still working on his first shower. John asked if the man could sign Frank's log as witness to his run. Such record-keeping was imperative for Frank's claim of a world record. The man obliged and was on his way.

There was no ideal explanation for the meeting, even decades later. Frank simply lacked the time or interest to wonder if the guy actually was finishing his own coast-to-coast adventure. Frank saw no metaphorical connection to the simplicity of a man singularly completing a leisurely three thousand-mile walk and seemingly content, while Frank hurriedly headed three thousand miles in the opposite direction feeling crowded and conflicted.

"Our country is littered with folks coming and going," Frank said later, "sometimes homeless."

Winds from thirty to fifty miles per hour and the desert heat started to conspire against Frank. He felt lightheaded, an early sign of bonking, that punch-drunk running feeling caused by a loss of energy through the depletion of glycogen stores in the liver and muscles. Sugar typically reversed the symptoms, but John was out of sweets and the motor home, supposed to be 2½ miles ahead, continued past the meeting point, unable to find a secure spot to pull over. Frank finally caught up to his crew and downed candy and fruit juice. Disaster averted.

The first day came to an end a few minutes before eight at night near Vallejo at the intersection of Interstate 80 and American Canyon Road. The opening-day numbers: eleven hours, ten minutes, fifty-five miles. The support crew found a campground ten miles away in Vallejo, meticulously charting the landmark where Frank finished so the crew could return to that point in the morning. They ate dinner and showered before Frank's dad began the first of many deep massages up and down his son's body.

Frank couldn't imagine getting across the country without them. Of course, Sonny's expertise, honed as a male nurse, wouldn't produce miracles. The massages allowed Frank to keep running and enjoy a semblance of comfort. Pain would be his constant training partner.

Frank had finished one day in his quest to break the world record for fastest run across America. He was shot. As bad as he had imagined the pain, it was worse. His entire body ached, his energy gone.

But Day Two would represent an early awakening and a defining moment.

5

His Father's Son

Two years after the birth of Frankie, as he was called during childhood, the Gianninos bought their first home, in the tiny Rockland County hamlet of Blauvelt, which has since grown to a whopping five thousand people.

Frankie had an uphill battle from birth. He was diagnosed with a lateral curvature of both feet and spent his first six weeks with full casts on both legs. The casts were replaced each week so his fragile bones could be realigned to the correct location. Frankie's feet finally began to develop properly at two months old.

Frank's dad worked in the psychiatric unit at Bellevue Hospital on First Avenue in Manhattan, the oldest public hospital in the country. He went to work at Rockland State Hospital, later known as Rockland Psychiatric Center, while working as the evening shift supervisor at Nyack Hospital.

He did what he needed to do to feed his family, which meant working two, sometimes three jobs to make ends meet during much of Frankie's youth. Sonny was a male nurse by day at Sing Sing Correctional Facility in Westchester County, and by night put in hours at Nyack Hospital. He paid off the home mortgage in half the allotted time, yet money was a common source of arguments between the couple. What had more of an impact, though, was the unspoken lack of affection witnessed by the oldest boy.

"I rarely saw them hug," Frank said of his parents. "It was always a larger person with a smaller person; he was 5'6" and she was 5'7" and overweight. There was not open affection. As the years go by, I think that happens a lot in relationships."

Frank had a typical blue-collar upbringing in many ways. His dad, a former church usher, was a practicing Catholic – "devout" might have been too strong a description – and Ruth converted from Protestant to Catholicism when they married. They raised the children Catholic and made sure they had Christian educations in grade school.

The Giannino kids lacked some of the perks of their peers. Family vacations were quite rare. Their biggest outings involved visiting family members in upstate New York. Frankie's most exotic vacation was a road trip to the New Jersey Shore when he was seven or eight.

"It wasn't abnormally dysfunctional," is how his sister Barbara described their family life.

The children had a good childhood, loosely defined in the 1950s and '60s as getting along without being abused by your parents. But there was deep-ridden, unspoken conflict. And what better poster child for inner turmoil than Frank, the walking smile, the showman who would catch snakes for his backyard aquarium and dangle them at his oldest sister Marijean and her friends for attention. It earned him the nickname "Snake Boy" by age eleven.

"He made things interesting," youngest sister Nancy said. "He wasn't a boring person. He had a lot of charisma, but he was always withdrawn at the same time. He always did stuff different. He still does stuff different."

Frank had enough presentable clothes and shoes, enough toys and sporting outlets such as Little League, to keep pace with peers and avoid the outcast's cocoon. Yet he felt a sense of darkness and emptiness colored by insecurity growing up. Frank quickly took sides in family squabbles. He was his father's son.

Frank and his dad held a deep bond, a source of frustration for Mom and special resentment from Marijean. She was devastated when Frank was born, seeing him as one more obstacle in the strained relationship with her father. Marijean didn't feel she received the same affection from Dad as Frank, and could never understand why Frank put his dad on a pedestal. She called Frank a "scatterbrain."

"She so resented him," Barbara said. "We went to the hospital with my father to pick up Mom and (Frank). I remember my sister's first comment was, 'He's a really ugly baby.' She was always going on about him. He could do no right."

Later, while attending the State University of New York at Oneonta, Marijean and her mom spent large chunks of trips to the school trashing Dad, who was critical of Marijean as well. Nancy remembered her dad not hesitating to comment when Marijean gained weight. Marijean's rocky relationship with her father only intensified her bitterness toward Frank. Dad and son would leave their home at four a.m. on fishing trips to the famed Roscoe streams up in Northern Sullivan County, New York. Dad claimed Frank brought him luck, the highlight when Frank caught his first Rainbow trout. Dad coached Frank in Little League as well.

Nancy shared no such bitterness toward Frank. She was a tomboy and palled around with him. Nancy and Frank bonded despite his being more than three years older. They hung out, sometimes together, sometimes in their own groups, down by the churning creek near their home. They were always in the middle of something, almost drowning one winter day while trying to retrieve a Chinese tea cup that had fallen into the frozen stream. Both siblings fell into the creek and Nancy grabbed hold of a log to stay above water.

She was his sidekick when he needed one. Frank taught Nancy how to catch snakes by grabbing them right behind the head. Nancy's own sense of adventure landed her in trouble on occasion. She was barely in kindergarten when she got her hand stuck in one of those old-fashioned cigarette machines with the trays on the bottom. She escaped serious injury at seven despite falling off an elephant at a local fair.

"I was probably the most defiant of the five of us," Nancy said. "I was a great liar. I could look my mother in the eye and lie. Frankie was always my hero. We confided in each other."

Frank tried to keep Nancy out of trouble, though she said it was "his match" that set a former golf course on fire. As he matured, Frank yearned to have the same qualities as his dad, mostly his confidence, organization skills and work ethic. Frank, however, had one unique characteristic from all others in his immediate family. The kid was habitually upbeat.

"People would be like, 'Why is he so happy about things when they are falling apart?'" Barbara said.

Frank's knee-jerk smile, however, belied his self-doubt. He was great at hiding his true feelings.

"I always find myself with self-doubt; (my father) was extremely positive about everything," Frank said. "I've never met a more confident individual. Literally the most hard-working guy I've ever seen in my life.

"And Dad was so good at letting things go. It was hard for me not to care what people thought. I tried a lot to be like him letting things roll off my shoulders, being confident."

Yet Frank maintained somewhat of a flawed view of his dad as a heroic figure. Frank's father was fairly cynical. He was typical of many fathers during that time: set in his ways, emotionally unpredictable and detached. He dealt with conflict through avoidance. The characteristic might have stemmed from before Frank was born, when Marijean, maybe four at the time, spilled something at the dinner table. Dad went to grab her and wound up accidentally pushing her off her chair. Marijean was okay, but the incident shook her father.

From that point on, the kids would fight with each other and Dad chose to let Ruth settle it. Barbara remembered him coming home to a spirited fight between herself and Marijean, only to immediately turn around and leave. He kept things bottled up until occasional rousing outbursts.

There was the time he put a fist through two pieces of sheet rock out of frustration over the kids bickering.

"He was not the disciplinarian," Barbara said. "Marijean cracked up the car once and he didn't say a word. But he hit the wall (at home) and put a hole in it. Who was stuck with all the bad things? Mom. Dad didn't deal with it."

6

Disappointing Dad

Frank already needed to dig deeply into his physical and mental reserve on Day Two. He lacked the long list of multi-day event numbers that show up on an ultra-marathoner's dossier. An ultra-running foundation, after all, provides the experience of dealing with all kinds of adverse situations, from intense pain to nagging mental battles.

Frank, however, did possess the ultra-runner's superior mental strength. He knew how to channel negatives into positives, how to ease pain through focus, creative thinking and visualization.

Tomato fields lined the route just outside of San Francisco, allowing Frank to channel his inner Italian and see them freshly turning into sauce at Shakey's Pizza, where he had worked part-time while in the Army stationed in Anchorage, Alaska. He thought of how he worked in front of the restaurant window performing for kids poking their noses against the glass. Ever the showman, Frank was at his goofy best doing silly little dances or juggling pans or flipping dough in front of the children.

There was one problem, however, with Frank's nostalgic trip. He wasn't the only Giannino presently lost in something. His dad, determinedly steering the motor home, was lost in a more literal sense.

The parties had been separated by a road divider, with Frank and John going one way and Sonny going the other. In another era, an easy call or text would have solved the problem. In 1980, such separations could spell major problems. Frank knew better than most, having endured the nightmare of Run One when he and Billy Glatz were so thoroughly lost that their handler, Becky Wright, contacted State Police, who in turn posted an all-points bulletin on the running duo.

It led to Frank incorporating a safeguard on this trip in case he was separated from the support vehicle. He instructed his dad to find the next intersection and stay put. If the groups failed to reunite in a reasonable period of time, Frank was to call the State Police.

Sonny, meantime, was getting anxious. He calculated the length of time when Frank and John had been gone – about ten minutes – and figured they were, at most, a mile away. But that didn't ease the father's concern. He was approaching full-fledged panic when a police officer saw the "Run Across America" banner on the motor home and stopped to ask if they were looking for a runner.

"Come on," the officer told Sonny, offering an escort, "I know where they are."

Safely reunited with their family, Frank and John approached a drawbridge that would take them into Sacramento when John suffered his first flat tire. He rushed the bike to the motor home ahead, latched it to the back and headed on foot over the bridge with his big brother.

Bruce had made plans with United Way officials and the media to meet Frank in the city. But only a lone photographer greeted the runners on the bridge to snap photos. When Frank and John came off the bridge, there was no reception. Perhaps, Frank said, their half-hour tardiness scattered the party.

Oh well, Frank wasn't about to let a near-bonking experience, excruciating full-body pain, support-team separation and a publicity snafu ruin the opening two days of his cross-country run. Not Frank.

He was fully capable of ruining the run himself.

Frank had, indeed, run clear across the United States of America once already. He had planned for his second run as thoroughly as possible for a guy who spent most of his waking days living in the moment. But Frank still had a lot to learn about long-distance running, if not running in general.

On Day Four he was climbing U.S. 50 to Lake Tahoe, a large freshwater lake in the Sierra Nevadas near the border between California and Nevada, when Frank came upon a trout pond by the side of the road. Frank's legs and feet ached from running fifty miles, mostly uphill. The pond was simply too inviting for Frank to ignore without, well, getting his feet wet. He removed his socks and shoes and dipped his legs into the pond, figuring the water would have a soothing, perhaps even blister-healing, effect.

"I had no idea," Frank said.

Frank's dad pulled up in the motor home with a less-than-soothing critique.

"Get your feet the hell out of there!" he yelled to his son.

Frank's father knew better. Water has a stiffening effect on muscles by constricting the blood vessels. It had precisely the opposite effect of what Frank sought. He immediately got up and felt a numb stiffness below his knees. Frank managed to walk a quarter-mile but couldn't run the rest of the day. He still wasn't quite right the following day.

Frank wasn't the only one enduring on-the-job training in the grueling pace of running across the country. His dad and step-mom were feeling their own multi-tasking pain and pressure of engineering a support team.

It wasn't the first time his dad had gotten angry with Frank. One of Frank's saddest childhood memories was when his dad, sick of the boy strumming his acoustic guitar and singing in the family's unfinished basement late one night, slammed the instrument against a metal pole that was helping support the foundation. The guitar, which the parents had bought for his twelfth birthday, crumbled into pieces.

"The first time I ever saw him angry," Frank said. "And the guilt he felt over that. 'Frankie,' I remember him saying, 'I told you to stop.'"

Guilt ran thick in the family. Dad felt so bad at his rant that he replaced the guitar with a sparkling new electric guitar. Music became another symbol of Frank's self-esteem issues. He was a backup vocalist and rhythm guitarist in a pre-teen garage band called "The Teenagers." They started to play in front of crowds, with Frank briefly taking to cigarettes and joining fellow band members in wearing black pants and boots and blue puffy shirts with puffy sleeves ala Tom Jones. Sonny called Frank's footwear his "Beatnik boots."

They performed at a junior high talent show and a junior high dance before Frank quit.

"It was the last time we played," Frank said. "I remember the two of the shows being the scariest moments of my life."

7

A Mountain (Bike) of Mistakes

Frank's entire body ached through the first five days. One of his few pleasures came on Day Three running past Folsom (California) Prison, which was the setting for the 1979 movie "The Jericho Mile" based on an inmate training for the Olympics. Frank had been instantly drawn to his first run when, in Magdalena, New Mexico, during a rare night's hotel stay, he came across the movie on TV. The movie helped pique Frank's interest in helping the inmate population, and a couple years later, he would organize 10Ks inside three prisons near home.

For now, though, Frank was starting to feel like a prisoner in his own body. Frank already was behind schedule, clocking daily mileage in the fifties. He would have to step it up big time, and soon, to have a shot at besting Cottrell.

Frank, again, wasn't the only one feeling the heat. The entire party started to feel the pressure. Tension began to mount.

Frank grew concerned with Sonny and Ja spending extra time finding campgrounds in which to stay overnight. Campgrounds allowed the family fresh water supplies and a hook-up to electrical services. But Frank knew there would be long stretches without the benefit of camping locales. He fought the ever-present temptation to grow discouraged over his struggles to average sixty miles a day.

Frank and his team completed crossing the first of twelve states and began their ritual of taking a family photo under the sign designating the state they were entering. They moved into

Nevada and Bruce snapped off a picture of them under a "Welcome to Nevada" sign. Frank's dad wasn't especially keen on Nevada, calling it the "armpit of the world." His crude ranking system related directly to the state's accessibility to water for drinking and supplying the motor home. One of the forgotten challenges of running across the country was going long stretches without the convenient availability of water.

Frank finally accomplished his first sixty-miler on Day Six. But it came at a price. He felt intense diaphragm soreness.

"There was pain every day," he said. "It never stopped. I just ignored it and kept pushing. Ultra distance legend Marshall Ulrich said it best: 'Pain is a learned experience. You can manage it.'"

Frank's bubbly personality and **relentless** optimism came in especially handy when discomfort pierced his body. Instead of being disappointed with the slow start and burdened by the pain, Frank felt a burst of confidence after his first sixty-mile day. He knew he could run longer. In fact, Frank thought he could stretch it out to seventy-mile days. Sure enough, he started to consistently clock daily sixty-plus milers.

"After the first week, we started to pick it up," he said. "There was better planning."

By Day Eight, Frank felt excruciating pain in his left shin. He adjusted his orthotics and wrapped his shins with a second larger surgical hose, which essentially served as athletic tape keeping his muscles tight and intact. But the shin pain brought about another setback. Frank had only forty-six miles in him for the day. It was just the type of injury to keep him off world-record pace.

The night showed promise. They ate in a restaurant and Frank called an ex-girlfriend, Michele Aparisi, to soften his mood. The attraction had been immediate after meeting the previous spring at a bar in New Paltz called McGuinn's Village Inn. They found each other interesting and she was especially supportive of Frank's run. When Frank got off the phone, Sonny went to work on Frank's shin to lessen its swell.

"Bruce," Frank shouted from his bunk, "why don't you get your guitar?"

Bruce complied. He strummed the guitar and started to sing. Frank joined in, providing a melodic finish to a painful day.

The problem with music is that even the most remarkable tune has a final note. Then it's off to the bitter chords of reality, unable to click the playback button that matches a song with a tender moment. For Frank, and perhaps most others, songs are connected to heartbreak and disappointment, like Rod Stewart's "Maggie May" bizarrely popping from his car radio every ten minutes during a deflated trip home after being spurned by his first love at her summer place in New England nine years earlier.

You led me away from home,
just to save you from being alone
You stole my heart
and that's what really hurt ...

The friendship with Michele came four years after Frank's crushing loss, the split with Patty Whelan. Frank and Patty were supposed to have been a permanent couple by now. At least that's how Frank saw it. She saw it another way, crushing his ego, leaving him confused and vulnerable, rejected and dejected. Michele helped restore his faith in women. But he wondered if he had chased away his lifelong partners. When was he going to be able to choose his own song as a groom? When would an artist's perfect notes bring pleasure and promise instead of pain and regret?

The eighth-day sing-along turned into a ninth-day medley of pain. Frank tried to find his form, but his left shin howled like coyotes in Nevada's morning dark. Every step was met with torturous pain in his leg.

Frank needed to do something to relieve his agony. He fiddled with his orthotics again. Frank used a Morton's Extension, a tight carbon foot orthotic that extends to the tip of the big toe. The extension tightened the area while giving his remaining toes the freedom to maneuver properly. Morton's Extension would become popular in years ahead for treating turf toe, a common football injury. For now, it was a remarkable remedy for Frank's cross-country toe.

Frank used flat Spenco neoprene on both shoes. He took the right pad and cut out an area under four toes and four balls of his forefoot, leaving an extension in his big toe and raising his foot.

Frank started to feel relief almost immediately. He was back to running relatively comfortably and pain free. Frank's dad and Ja, meanwhile, drove into Eureka, Nevada, to find medical help for Sonny's cramps and diarrhea. The town is located along U.S. Highway 50 which, for reasons clear to the entire party, is nicknamed "The Loneliest Road in America." The nearest town along the highway, Austin, is seventy miles away. But Sonny and Ja discovered a clinic in Eureka – Eureka! – and Sonny was prescribed medication. He still felt like shit, but by the time Frank and John caught up to them, Frank had little time for sympathy or nurturing. There was room for only one suffering participant. He had to keep running.

They met up again a few miles later to break for lunch. Frank headed for the bathroom and was in the middle of his duty when Sonny turned on the motor home to find a better parking spot. Before John had a chance to break the news, the sound of metal on metal rang out.

"Jesus H. Christ, John!" Sonny shouted to the teenager. "How many times do I have to tell you? I can't see your bike when you park it in front of the motor home."

"I thought we were going to stay here a while," John mumbled.

John stepped out of the vehicle as Sonny and Frank followed. The shiny $400 Fuji lay in tatters.

Frank figured it was as good a time as any to start running again. "You guys figure out how to get another bike," he said. "For now, I'll just have to move without John's immediate help. Don't worry, you guys. I'm going to get some food in me right now. I'm feeling pretty good. My overall soreness is not as bad as it was. I'll see you up the road as soon as you can."

Frank ate quickly and headed up the road. Sonny was furious, John devastated.

The support team went into town trying to find another bike. Bruce had an idea. "When we get to Ely, he said of the town seventy-seven miles away, "I'll call the radio station. I'll tell them about Frank's run and what has happened to John's bike. Maybe that will bring something."

Sonny was hardly optimistic. He already was skeptical of Bruce's public relations acumen in particular and competence in general. "I doubt it," Sonny replied.

The bike accident and friction between Sonny and Bruce had left the group in a dour mood as they settled in for dinner. Frank knew the crucial role John played in the run. But John would have a heck of a time guiding his big brother without a bicycle.

The team headed for Ely later that day. Sonny and Ja found a motel, figuring it a much-needed respite from the frustrations of the previous day. Frank finished within five miles of Ely. The crew marked the spot of Frank's finish with the orange bike flag from John's mangled ride, then headed to the motel.

When Frank arrived, Bruce stood excitedly at the motel entrance. He led Frank to his room, where in the middle stood a ten-speed bicycle. Son of a gun. Bruce's calls to radio stations had worked. A brewery owner named William Cooper heard the announcement in a nearby town and donated the bike.

It was no Fuji, or any other name brand, for that matter. It was a Montgomery Ward AAU bike, not exactly the preferred symmetry to Frank's AAU shoes. But nobody, not even Sonny, was about to complain.

Frank had his riding companion back in the fold. Now he desperately needed to start churning out seventy-mile days.

8

Support from the Iron Man

Frank awoke to major muscle soreness in his arms, midsection and quads. About the only parts of his body that didn't hurt were his calves, perhaps the result of reducing stride length and wearing compression hose on both legs. His ego remained quite healthy as well. It was Day Eleven, more than a month to the finish, but a pivotal day in Frank's quest for the world record.

First he needed a fix from Dad, curator of the miracle massage. Cashing in on a course for massage in nursing school, Sonny knew precisely the muscles to stimulate and the method of execution. He would give his son three massages a day – before and after lunch, and after dinner. Frank, his feet often numb, lay on his stomach as his dad began gently massaging each toe to the bottom of Frank's foot. With long strokes, the father worked his son's Achilles' tendons, calves, hamstrings and soft tissue on the back of Frank's legs, then his lower back. Dad worked the lactic acid toward Frank's heart, which would help filter the material from his body through the kidneys.

Frank felt like a million bucks and set out for his early run. His father was cranky at times, but he could have earned a living as a masseuse. The family posed under the "Welcome to Utah" sign and Frank finished the day a few miles later.

The day of his life.

Frank had clocked his first seventy-miler, going 70.8 miles into Utah on U.S. 50, his final five miles, as he put it, "moving right along."

"I was frustrated that I hadn't met a seventy-mile day," he said. "I knew once I got there, I was going to keep getting there. I knew then that I was going to own the record."

Frank was just getting started. He completed 70.2 miles the next day, which would be remembered for two reasons. It was the first of his twelve days on the road without encountering pain at some point. And John showed off his superb touch in the all-important area of music selection.

The teen flipped into his boom box a cassette of Eddie Rabbitt's "Drivin' My Life Away." Frank, however, vociferously manipulated the lyrics.

Ooh I'm RUNNIN' my life away
looking for a better way for me

At last, a pleasant song.

There are only a handful of guarantees to running across the country. One is meeting an eclectic band of people. Frank was running uphill toward Fruitland, Utah, when a local runner appeared from the shadows to join him. They struck up a conversation and Frank, being Frank, invited the guy and his wife to the motor home that night. Ralph promised to bring his wife Linda to visit after dinner. Soon Ralph and Linda were meeting the Gianninos.

John looked upon his brother's gesture with curiosity. The guy could be crazy, maybe a mass murderer, John suggested. But Frank was struck by Ralph's unique running gait, like a duck in full waddle. Frank related to Ralph's sense of adventure and need to discover peace and simplicity in a world of noise and complexity.

Ralph, a Los Angeles native, met Linda after moving to Seattle. Ralph did a little construction and other odd jobs, but he was restless and needed to experience the serenity of the mountains. So he moved Linda out of Seattle and away from her family. They settled down in a trailer in Utah.

But Ralph had ignored a crucial element in the equation: Linda.

Linda sniffed out an accommodating ear inside the motor home. "Does he care? No," Linda told Ja. "He just keeps going on and on about the beauty and the fresh air of the damn mountains. You'd think he was married to these mountains. Spends more time with them than he does with me, that's for sure."

"Sure, you want to go back to crime and muggings, polluted water and air, constant noise, constant tension," Ralph said. "I couldn't take it again, not after the peace I've known here."

"Yeah, like 'Rest in Peace,'" Linda huffed. "I might as well be dead living here."

Ralph and Linda signed the log register and finally went on their way.

"They certainly were an odd couple," Ja said, as if 'odd' could be accurately defined anymore inside the motor home.

The family called it a night. Three in the morning would arrive quickly. Frank was close to reaching Colorado, a piece of the run that would live with him forever.

If only he could find some comfort in his AAU shoes. Sonny had been working on them from the start, soaking the forefoot of each shoe in an attempt to widen them for a more comfortable fit. Sonny needed a shoe stretcher to enlarge them properly, but their travels didn't wind through strip malls and specialty stores. They were lucky to find enough water for drinking and bathing, no less locating a technical shoe instrument such as a stretcher.

That wouldn't stop them from trying. Sonny, Ja and Bruce drove into Craig, Colorado, in a desperate search for a stretcher. They came upon a Thom McAn shoe store, where Sonny quickly spotted a wooden shoe stretcher used by employees.

The manager told Sonny that the stretcher was a store item and not for sale. Sonny first chose diplomacy, explaining that his son was trying to set a world record for the fastest run across the U.S.

Great, the manager said, but what does that have to do with wanting a shoe stretcher?

Having failed with diplomacy, Sonny went to Plan B: firmness.

"He has a wide forefoot," Sonny said. "He's running about seventy miles per day. His shoes need an effective widening tool. The toe box of his shoes needs that tool so his feet have more room. His forefeet are constantly numb. Again, he needs that tool now. We are in a race against time. I don't have the time for a place that sells them retail. I'm already late for the next rendezvous point with him. So please, how much do you want for that thing?"

"Since this is a very special case, I'll let you have it for $10," the manager said finally.

Frank had covered 1,080 miles and was averaging sixty per day. His plan was to average at least sixty miles through the mountains. They celebrated with a rare meal out, and at an Italian restaurant no less. Frank called Michele Aparisi again to share the beauty and experiences of the run. But really, he just wanted to hear her voice.

What Frank didn't want to hear was his dad's voice in agony. Sonny had started to feel ill with diarrhea and stomach cramps by the end of the first week. Frank was momentarily jolted. He had never seen his dad sick. He worried about Sonny hitting his own wall. But Frank was so focused on the task at hand that he quickly redirected his concentration to the run. Such was the selfishness required of the cross-country runner. Stressing over things you couldn't control amounted to wasted energy.

But it was another reminder that successful runs across America depend upon the health of the support team as much as they do the runner. Frank could try to ignore the distraction all he wanted. But one unhealthy member of the team, no less a cog as crucial as Frank's dad, could destroy the mission.

Sonny recovered from his stomach problems, but he started experiencing another tenuous moment physically. This one, thankfully, possessed a humorous footnote. Sonny continued to spend hours working on Frank's shoes to make them as comfortable as possible. Frank's feet took a special pounding on the downhill portions of the Rocky Mountain runs in Colorado. Sonny soaked the shoes, stretched them and used Shoe Goo, an adhesive product, to replace worn areas on the heel. Then he would hang the finished shoes to dry on prongs of the bicycle rack at the front of the motor home. Sonny was finishing up a pair when he started to feel lightheaded.

"I wonder if it's the medication," he told Ja, referring to his medication taken earlier for the stomach issues.

"Could be, or maybe it's from the elevation," Ja said. "We keep going up and down all the time. The elevation might be affecting you."

Sonny started to get a case of the giggles. "Yeah, it's probably the elevation or the medication." He giggled again. "Doesn't feel so bad though."

Sonny discovered another phenomenon. "Do you know what's funny?" he asked Ja. "When I start to get lightheaded, my ass gets numb."

"Your what?" she said.

"My ass gets numb. Don't suppose that's from the elevation, do you?"

They decided that it must be from the medication, but Sonny continued giggling while performing shoe surgery on Frank's kicks.

"What are you giggling about?" Ja asked.

"I don't know. I must really be getting giddy."

John walked in for a break from biking and wondered what was so funny. He picked up a container of Shoe Goo and read the label aloud: "Not to be used in confined areas."

With the source of Sonny's giggles discovered, he decided it might be best to use the Shoe Goo outside.

At least Sonny had the modest accommodations of the motor home. When you are trying to get across the country in record-breaking time, you don't spend precious minutes searching for a public restroom. You go when you need to go. Frank's bowel movements were often carried out on the sides of roads, sometimes no more than a couple feet from the highway. Earlier in the run, he unleashed an especially vigorous release after foolishly ingesting five plums. Live and learn.

But heading through Poudre Canyon, a narrow, glacier-formed valley about forty miles long in Larimer County,

Colorado, brought Frank another reminder of a different battle between man and nature. He was moving along quite well when he ran into a camera crew filming a documentary on the beauty of the canyon and its wildlife. The crew explained that they were chronicling the government's insistence on building a dam and turning the canyon into a reservoir.

The crew's goal wasn't all that different from Frank's. They wanted to share the government's intentions with the masses. Frank wanted to share his own intentions with the masses. He wanted to be acknowledged for performing an exceptional feat.

Yet Frank wasn't so caught up in chasing his goal that he ignored the surroundings. He had a great fondness for nature, and no state excited him more than Colorado.

"To me, the magical moment was near Cameron Pass on the twenty-first day," he said. "It's the highest point of the run at over ten thousand feet. It was a religious moment for me because I felt like I was in church. There are large granite boulders surrounding you and it takes your breath away. For me, everything seemed downhill from there."

He meant the terrain, not the experience. Located sixty-five miles north of Denver, Fort Collins is situated at the base of the Rocky Mountain foothills. Frank, who has never met a mountain he didn't want to climb, was captivated by the pure beauty of the region.

On a broader scope, he equated the mountains of the West to his running upbringing on the world-renowned Shawangunk Mountains back in the Hudson Valley. Frank felt at home in the Rockies.

He loved everything about the West, the smell, the peaks. Wanting to reach the top was always a fascination. If you stripped Minnewaska State Park, located along the northern ridge of the Shawangunks, of all the trees, it would look like the landscape out West.

Frank's seventeen-year-old brother wasn't viewing the land with similar depth. The Rockies presented one of John's more stressful periods as he experienced severe leg cramps pedaling through the mountains. For two days, John biked two miles and walked a mile, eventually recovering on his way down the mountain. He called the descent "a beautiful ride down the hill."

John was along for the ride in the most literal sense, trying to help his brother reach a goal, missing a little school, doing something different. Naturally his mind occasionally wandered to one compelling thought: *What in the world am I doing out here?*

On some occasions, John had a single pressing thought: sleep. When the dreamy state arrived, as it did on this day, John simply stopped a half-mile or so ahead of Frank, laid his bicycle on the side of the road and closed his eyes.

He began getting tired after the first couple days with the thrill of the adventure dissipating. The first week was exciting. The second week he found himself dozing early in the morning while on the bike.

John spent parts of the second and third weeks going ahead and finding places alongside the road for twenty-minute power naps. Being seventeen and all, the naps often took place carelessly alongside guard rails, which led to a few brushes with impatient truckers zooming a few feet past John's motionless body. A tractor trailer blew him completely off the bike near Nevada, leaving a few bruises behind. He dusted himself off, ignored the minor scrapes, and carried on. Another time in the thick of night, Frank darn near stepped on John's head as he slept, not seeing him until the last second.

"John, what the hell are you doing?' Frank said. "What if a semi came along before me? You'd be dead, you idiot."

John, fast becoming the support-team whipping boy, mumbled something about taking a little nap. He wished the road's shoulder were his bed back home in Walden. John couldn't pedal up especially steep hills. So he walked the bike up the high rises like a little kid who had strayed too far from home.

There were times when John got a later start and caught up with Frank on the roads. But John had the ideal temperament pedaling shotgun with Frank. The boy found a rhythm and his own method of disassociation. He simply stopped analyzing the challenges and plowed ahead.

Unlike his big brother, John reached the point where he stopped thinking about the challenge. The mind set allowed him to keep from getting overwhelmed. After a couple weeks, he got used to the routine and focused on fulfilling Frank's directives. He knew Frank didn't want to deal with the "itty-bitty bullshit," and that included worrying about his teenaged brother holding up his end.

The rest of the crew came to truly appreciate John's effort. His pedaling endurance led to the family tagging him with a nickname: Iron Man.

Frank admired his brother's perseverance and lack of drama. John was the perfect sidekick. He was never much into organized sports, especially track and field. John had lasted less than one season of track at Valley Central High near the family's Walden home. He didn't like the coach and quit. John was just never into running like his brother. Nor did he enjoy the organized element of sports. If he wanted to play football, he did so with his buddies on church property near his house.

John and Frank viewed their dad similarly. Never domineering or overbearing. Never verbally or physically abusive. "He was an ideal father to me," John said. "He never really got upset often. When he did, it was my fault."

The bond with their father helped explain John's bond with Frank. The brothers were too far apart in age, eleven years, to have a sibling rivalry. They were more friends, buddies, who placed no expectations or demands on one another. John was non-judgmental and a great listener. He looked at things clearly and objectively without any ulterior motive or agenda.

They shared a zest for adventure and travel, like the month during John's youth when they had hiked Yosemite for four days and camped in the shadow of El Capitan. He took a four-day bus trip to Flagstaff, Arizona, alone at age fourteen, to visit Frank during his college stop at Northern Arizona. They road-tripped to California to visit their oldest sister Marijean, hitting points along the way, then made their way up the West Coast, stopping at Lassen Volcanic National Park in northeastern California. The brothers hiked to the top of a volcano and ran downhill on the soft ashes, kicking up an avalanche with their strides.

"I was never at odds with my brother," John said. "Growing up, the age difference always put us in different places emotionally. The age difference probably helped us remain tight. We never competed for attention from my father. My father was more involved with my brother growing up, from what I understand. He pushed my brother more to excel."

So how much studying did John actually do during the run? How many books actually were opened? "I tried one day," he said. "I opened a physics book and did no work."

A few days after Dad's Shoe Goo incident, Frank noticed something during a rare stop in a luxurious public restroom. His dad might have gotten a numb ass from the Shoe Goo. But Frank had been reduced to possessing virtually "no ass" –not to mention an excruciatingly sore one – from one thousand-plus miles of road work. He used a rubber doughnut on the toilet seat for better cushion, but the damage had been done.

Frank had lost eighteen pounds, down to 147, since the start of the run.

"I look malnourished," he said to his family. "Can you imagine what I'll look like by the end of the run?"

Ja's Danishes, an early morning staple, could only produce so much excess energy for Frank. He needed more food despite ingesting about six thousand calories a day. Sonny insisted on increasing Frank's caloric intake. He eventually would ramp it up to ten thousand calories daily. "We'll just have to experiment until we find out what works," Frank said, as if it were the crew's first voyage into the uncertain world of experimentation.

Sonny had his own idea to add pounds to his son's bony body: milkshakes.

The plan was to consume a milkshake at the start of each of Frank's one-hour breaks during the day.

Frank approached the middle of the country on a roll. The crew finally had developed a structured daily itinerary. Ja got up first to make farina, a bland cereal food with wheat germ and honey, for Frank and John. Sonny converted his bed into a breakfast dining table. Frank and John would eat quickly and hit the road while Ja cleaned the breakfast mess, straightened the beds and made Danishes for snacks.

Sonny would drive ahead to the first three-mile checkpoint. Ja, Sonny and Bruce would run errands, do laundry and make public relations contacts leading to the twenty-five-mile stop for a full-fledged breakfast, often Ja's omelets. They broke for lunch at the fifty-mile point, typically sandwiches, soup, fruit and juices. Sonny massaged Frank at fifty miles and Frank would grab a quick nap, time permitting.

They performed a similar routine after lunch. If Sonny, Ja and Bruce were off doing their thing, John would provide snacks and water for himself and Frank. Ja used the time to prepare dinner that would coincide with Frank's final run of the day. She stirred sauces, mixed ingredients and baked entrees amid the bumps and turns of her ride. In the future era of virtually infinite television channels, she might have earned her own cooking show from the effort.

Sonny massaged Frank's entire body at the end of each day while Ja cleaned up after dinner.

All the amenities provided by his support team, though, couldn't solve Frank's foot issues. His ill-advised decision to soak his feet early in the run came back to bite him. Protective calluses had been replaced by painful blisters. Every step brought intense pain. All the while, Frank fought a similarly challenging mental battle. He talked openly about recognition – an occasional newspaperman here, a television reporter there – playing a key role in helping his frame of mind. But Frank continued to go long stretches without publicity. He ran by a television station in the northeastern Colorado town of Sterling. Nothing. A couple miles later, he jogged past a newspaper. Nothing.

Bruce was the convenient scapegoat, and he had one influential enemy: Sonny.

9

Far from the Best

The very first time Frank ran was before kindergarten at a Family Day near his home in Rockland County. The day was memorable for another reason. It was the first time he walked away from running with a feeling of disappointment.

Frank's legs moved slowly and he finished in the middle of a pack that included about twenty kids. The feeling was as much frustration as elation. How did he feel? He didn't win – that's how he felt. He wasn't as good as the other kids, is how he felt.

But he would have to get used to those feelings of inferiority.

Frank soon realized that he had one chance for running glory. He had to outlast the competition. He had to utilize any mechanism he could – intelligence, desire, heart, whatever – to wear down the field and finish first.

And so he did. Some of Frank's fondest running memories were blowing away neighborhood kids in the five-eighths of a mile loop around his block as a ten-, eleven- and twelve-year-old. He had no shot in the sprints. But he'd finish that loop with a head of steam while his peers gasped for air at the finish line.

The boy had running, but he also had a whole heap of issues transitioning from eighth grade in a Catholic school to freshman year at the public school Tappan Zee High. Cliques were being established and cemented, the popular and unpopular defined. Frank struggled to discover the self-confidence needed to develop friendships. He was hurrying to class with an armful of books on the first day of school when he collided with a passer-by. The books went flying and Frank started fighting with the boy, landing him an early invitation to the principal's office. Welcome to school, kid.

He especially felt inadequate around girls. Frank coped with his insecurities by developing an attitude. He cursed a lot. He joined the drinking crowd. He started smoking cigarettes. Smoking seemed kind of cool. So Frank smoked about a pack and a half daily through most of his freshman year. He needed to become part of the crowd, any crowd. So he became a follower.

And he barely passed freshman year with a sixty-five average.

"I just never felt like I was the boss of anything," he said. "I don't think I was an angry kid. I was a frustrated kid."

Ruth Giannino saw the nervous energy in Frank and suggested he try track. Frank did his best to stay with the lead pack during a three-lap time trial on the first day of practice. But he wound up in the back, and when he eventually crossed the finish line, Frank found a patch of grass next to the track and vomited.

"That first week of running on a team," he said, "was the most incredible week of my life. I was in awe of the upperclassmen on the team. They were all good runners. I was inspired by each one and eventually came to respect, even love, my teammates."

He just tried to survive in the beginning. Three weeks after the time trial, Frank ran his first high school race, the 880-yard run. He finished last of five runners and walked to the infield feeling lightheaded. Frank lay on his back to recover and peered up at the bright blue sky when suddenly a familiar voice came from above. It was Sonny Giannino, who had been expected to miss the meet because of work.

"You must feel like you've run a hundred miles, son," he said.

Actually more like three thousand.

Frank continued running. He wasn't so much running from his problems as he was running to figure them out. Running was his life preserver when everything around him seemed muddied and complicated. By now he had moved on from the unhealthy crowd, realizing some of his friends were bad influences. Frank would go on to increase his running load to forty-five to fifty miles a week by the end of his freshman year.

He entered a two-miler as his second race that year. For whatever reason, everything came together on a scorching day at nearby Nyack High. He finished second to the county champ – while chewing gum, no less – and his coach placed an admiring arm around Frank's shoulder. Boy, did that feel good. He finally had succeeded. He finally had been noticed.

"It was the first time in my life I had a sense of purpose," he said. "The freedom, movement, athleticism, competitiveness. I loved having a row of my teammates cheering for me as I came off of each lap."

He whittled his two-mile time to 10:27 by the end of spring track. But Frank preferred cross country. He fell for the sport's beauty, the ruggedly hilly courses, many through woodsy areas, that reunited him with nature. Frank especially loved the longer distances of cross country. He started to experience the magic of maximum effort by extending himself on runs. Frank started feeling a sense of comfort in his own skin for the first time in his life.

Meantime, his dad endured his own grueling schedule working two jobs. Sonny reached his crossroads on the side of a road, exhausted by the work day, falling asleep at the wheel.

He suffered minor injuries. But he got the hint. Sonny got transferred to a Hudson Valley facility in luscious Ulster County called Wallkill Prison, later known as Wallkill Correctional Facility, and moved the family upstate the summer following Frank's freshman year at Tappan Zee High. The Gianninos settled nearby in the Village of Walden, Orange County, an hour north of Blauvelt, where they took up residence in a one-acre home on Riverview Street. Dad carved a huge "G" into the front shutters while Frank tried to carve his place in a different environment, still navigating the distance between awkwardness and acceptance.

Walden, like Blauvelt, was a tiny, intensely blue-collar town, described by sister Nancy as "a Little Rascals neighborhood." Frank discovered the outdoorsy perks to country living with the

Wallkill River as a backdrop, a tributary of the Hudson distinct for its northerly flow, merely one hundred and fifty feet from his doorstep.

"We went out on row boats, canoes," Frank said. "It was a very comfortable place."

At least Walden became a comfortable place. For a young teen dipping his toes in a pool of strangers, the move was terrifying.

Frank was still trying to adjust when tragedy struck. His mom was diagnosed with breast cancer.

Frank became one of the better schoolboy distance runners in the county as a sophomore at Valley Central High School near Walden. His self-esteem inched forward. Frank had ample room for improvement, but he was starting to kind of like himself.

That sophomore year included a flash of light from the Valley. Frank found himself running blistering workouts. The kid was a tremendous practice player who could hang with most anybody in dual meets.

Then darkness.

Frank powerfully prepared to face the best of the best in the big meets, the showdowns against rivals and season-ending championship events. But he couldn't beat the big boys. Frank got so worked up during races that he'd find himself uncharacteristically out of breath approaching the finish line. He came up short every single time in big meets. Frank knew the source of his problem, and he couldn't figure out what to do about it.

He was a choker.

"I sucked in big meets," he said. "It was like I was caught in the ocean and couldn't swim back to shore."

Frank was good enough to find acceptance outside of running. He joined pals walking across a beam supporting a bridge sixty feet above the Wallkill River. They performed silly and stupid stunts that define adolescence, like the summer before junior year when Frank and five buds ran through their neighborhood buck naked. They culminated the adventure by hopping uninvited into Mr. Sherman's pool, and soon were drying off at the police station.

The crew acted up in a barn behind Frank's house. They converted a horse-and-buggy barn into a two-tiered twenty-two-by fourteen-foot clubhouse brilliantly called "Frankie's Barn." Darkness was met by the twisting pop of beer caps against the rattle of unbuckling belts. This was where Frank, about to enter his junior year, made his first major move on a girl, his hand around a shoulder and sliding coyly to her chest.

Frank finally started getting serious about school as a senior. He made the honor roll for the first time. He started collecting books. He became an avid reader of Runner's World magazine.

And he became one of the leaders of the track team.

Frank started viewing running as much a journey as an activity. The summer before senior year, he had made his longest run with a couple friends, Bob Schmitt and Joe Schmidt, a seventeen-miler from Walden to coach Gene Martin's home a few towns over. Frank felt fresh upon arrival as he sucked in the adrenaline of accomplishment.

He was a month from high school graduation when he finally put it all together in a big meet. Frank found himself in the lead at the gun lap of the two-mile state track qualifier. He finally was going to beat the best runners in the entire section. Frankie was still winning the race with one hundred meters left when he was passed by two of the top dogs and finished third.

He would go on to flop at the state meet. But Frank felt a sense of fulfillment by his performance in the qualifier. His confidence soared.

The moment brought another startling appearance. Ruth Giannino was there to see her boy run in a meet for the first time. Her illness and duties at home had prevented Ruth from seeing Frank run throughout high school. Yet even with Mom there, even with the impressive finish, the scene that stuck with Frank Giannino revolved around visions of support and acceptance from others.

"What I remember forever is (former) teammates from Tappan Zee competing in the meet and Valley Central there cheering me," he said. "I was just in shock that I was leading all these guys."

"Frank," Coach Martin screamed when it was over, "you finally did it!"

"I never choked again," Frank said.

Maybe not, but even that breakthrough race had a hitch: Frank blew the lead in the final hundred meters. He still had yet to win the big one. He still was far from being the best.

10

Support Staff Loses a Member

Frank had become the last Giannino to defend Bruce Goldberg, the former newspaperman in charge of generating PR during the run. "It's not as easy as you think," Frank told John. "If we had an extra vehicle, we could freely promote this thing. A better communications system would help too. But we don't have these luxuries."

With the motor home as Bruce's only means of transportation, his contacts could not freely communicate with him. "He may leave a message for them, but then they cannot get back to him," Frank added. "So we lose opportunities. All he can do is keep trying to set things up. We'll just keep hoping for the best."

The run ground on. Frank clocked 63.2 miles during one agonizing day. Sonny pulled the motor home into the parking lot of a stock yard. Ja, meantime, managed to fit diary writing into her assorted duties.

Sept. 24: Colorado and Nebraska (to one mile west of Ogallala, Nebraska)
4 a.m.-8:10 p.m.
63.2 miles
Well, we're up a little later today, 3:20 a.m. I did not get dressed and cooked breakfast. Then I made Danish pastry after the first three-mile run. They were out of the oven after his next stop.

John got another flat tire on his bike. It's those little sputnik-type burrs that grow along the highway, the same things that Brindle picked up all over her paws. Frankie is losing both large toenails on his foot. They are very painful.

We are in Sedgwick. It is a small village. Bruce is making phone calls. We hurried back to pick up Frankie for breakfast. I started cooking breakfast while we were going to pick up Frankie. John got another flat. We picked him up and fixed it.

We stopped in Julesburg. John picked up some inner tubes for his bike and a couple of kits to repair his tires if he gets another flat. They are puncture-proof tubes, as this is a problem in this area.

We finally have crossed the border into Nebraska. We had our pictures taken in front of the sign. We stopped in Big Springs, did some laundry, got the soup and lunch for the boys and we are on our way.

We talked to (Frank's sister) Nancy. Driving down the road, we parked and two farmers stopped and gave us some miniature windmills. He said if we wanted more, he would send them to us no charge.

Frankie is losing both toenails. It is a painful process. He will lose one of them over the next two days. He ran today until 8:10 p.m. We drove up about a mile and parked for the night. We parked just outside of Ogallala. It is a stockyard for cattle. Across the road, the trains roar by all night and to our right is a small airport. We thought it would be a bad night between the cows mooing, the trains rushing by and sometimes a plane landing. We did not hear a thing once we fell asleep. We park in the most peculiar places. After supper, Sonny doctored Frankie's toes. He is taking good care of his feet. So another day has come to a close. The sunset was spectacular. Sonny took pictures.

Even the best-laid plan couldn't map out problems facing Frank and his team in Nebraska. Who knew that it was harvest season, leaving the smell of burning alfalfa positively nauseating Frank. Worse, Frank and John were forced to withstand the furious blitz of speeding trucks hurrying by to rush crops to their destinations. Dust and pollen filled the dry air making it difficult

71

for the brothers to breathe. And that burning alfalfa was making their stomachs churn.

John encountered the daunting challenge of trying to dodge the grain sifting out of trucks. The particles were like glass to bicycle tires, causing three flats in a single day that left John in need of another patch kit.

Inside the motor home, Ja met yet another challenge as the force of the trucks shook their vehicle. The burrs not only did a number on John's wheels, but made navigation for Brindle, Ja's beloved dog, especially perilous.

Bruce walked a different kind of tightrope trying to relate with Sonny. No matter how hard he tried, Bruce couldn't catch a break with Frank's dad. Sonny believed Bruce was doing a poor job generating publicity. It bugged Sonny that Bruce didn't devour Ja's meals. Frank's dad also had a problem with Bruce sometimes joining Frank on the road when, in Sonny's mind, Bruce should have been using every available minute to contact media outlets or help out in the motor home. Bruce had planned to run with Frank in each of the twelve states.

Bruce faced a daunting task as the only non-family member of the crew trying to live in close quarters with Frank's chain-smoking dad who couldn't stand him. By Nebraska, it had become clear that Bruce wasn't going to win over Sonny. The conflict was intensifying. It reached the point in which Sonny took issue with almost everything Bruce said or did. Even positive news from Bruce drew sarcasm from Frank's dad.

"It's about time," Sonny said when Bruce announced that a newspaper was sending reporters to interview Frank outside North Platte, Nebraska.

"I'm doing my best," Bruce said. "It's hard to contact people when you're always moving like this."

When Ja prepared one of Frank's favorites one night, meat loaf stuffed with Swiss cheese and wrapped in bacon, Bruce passed. When he wondered if Ja could perhaps "throw something together for him," a phrase Goldberg later said he never used, Sonny became outraged.

"No, Ja won't whip you up something," he said. "She's already made dinner. She does way too much as it is. If you don't like what Ja is making, don't eat it. There's plenty of food. Put something together and leave my wife alone."

Bruce grabbed fruit from the fridge and Frank tried to calm the situation. "That's enough, Dad," he said.

"Come on, Son," Sonny said finally, breaking the silence. "Let me take care of those toes."

Frank hated being in the middle of conflict, no less one involving his dad, and especially in the most important run of his life. But there was no avoiding it. If Sonny didn't like you, nothing was going to change his mind. It wasn't enough that Frank had to make peace when his dad and Bruce argued. Frank also was a sounding board for Bruce when he expressed his frustrations during their runs. The morning after their dinnertime blowout, however, John bore the brunt of Bruce's frustrations.

"John, your father, he's a little rough at times," Bruce said as he ran alongside John on his bike.

"He's alright," John said. "He worked many years with the inmate population. His fuse burns short sometimes."

"He is sure rough with me."

"You're just not used to him," John said.

Frank got a surge of adrenaline entering Grand Island. Only four months earlier, the city of Grand Island had been hit by seven tornados in a single evening, resulting in five deaths. A book written by Nebraska native Ivy Ruckman, *Night of the Twisters*, portrayed the disaster, and a television movie would be released years later loosely based on the book, centering on a family's battle to survive the night.

On this day, runners from the Grand Island Joggers Club joined Frank along the route. He needed the company. One toenail was completely ripped off and the other well on its way, his feet pockmarked with blisters. Still, United Way personnel, newspaper reporters and television crews from two local outlets provided Frank a jolt that helped him log a seventy-mile day.

Frank was on a roll, and son of a gun, so was Bruce. They received another United Way welcome in Omaha, with radio, TV and newspaper people chronicling the event while Frank and John, joined by a dozen runners, answered questions on the move. They were on the cusp of reaching the Missouri River and

Council Bluffs, Iowa. The next morning, they crossed the bridge into Council Bluffs – Frank wasn't bluffing when he insisted on crossing the span clearly marked with a "no pedestrian traffic" sign – to reach their sixth state. Frank was halfway home.

"Frankie's finally getting some recognition," Ja said after seeing the photo of Frank and John in the morning newspaper.

"It's about time," Sonny said, glancing at Bruce.

Later that day in Stuart, Nebraska, with Ja at the Laundromat, Sonny and Bruce went to pick up the guys along the road for breakfast. But they were nowhere in sight. Bruce thought Frank and John were up ahead. Sonny, having turned into a nagging contrarian involving all things Bruce, said there was no way the brothers could have gotten that far.

"I'm telling you, they had plenty of time to get that far," Bruce said.

"And I'm saying they couldn't have," replied an agitated Sonny, rising from his seat.

Ja, having joined in the search, played peacemaker and suggested they return to Stuart to ask around if anyone had seen the tandem. Bruce learned in a store that the pair had indeed gone by, proving him right. He returned to the motor home to report the news.

That only infuriated Sonny further. He told Bruce to keep his mouth shut. They found Frank and John at the intersection of I-80 and ate a late breakfast. A few hours later, Bruce pulled Frank aside as he wolfed down lunch.

"Frank," Bruce said, "when we get to Des Moines, I'm leaving."

"Why?" Frank said, knowing the answer.

"Your father. He threatened to kill me back there," Bruce said. "You can't tell him anything. I was right, anyway. You were ahead of us and he still wanted to punch me out."

"Bruce, there are only sixteen more days to the run," Frank said.

There was no changing Bruce's mind. It was bad enough that he couldn't please Frank's dad. Bruce's stomach problems were worsening. He had developed Giardia, an intestinal infection often caused by bad water and marked by stomach cramps, bloating, nausea and diarrhea. It was not a pleasant condition.

"I'm not going to live sixteen more days like this," he said. "He's liable to kill me. Sorry Frank."

"He's not going to kill you, Bruce."

"That's what you say. Besides, I'm not getting any better. I want to go home and see my own doctor."

"You sure this is what you want Bruce?" Frank said.

"I'm sure. I'm not getting anything out of this run anyway."

Sonny, stubborn as ever, had no interest in making peace with Bruce on the way out. The following day, United Way representatives met the crew near the West Des Moines city limit. Bruce spoke to one of the United Way officials and told Frank that the reps would take him to the airport.

He got out of the van as fast as he could with his luggage and got into the car. Bruce spent the night at the Des Moines YMCA and flew home the next day.

Frank had lost his public relations arm one month into the run. But he lost something greater. He lost a level of control over his run. Now he had to rely on his father, already loaded with responsibilities, to make media contacts as well. It was the last thing Frank needed to deal with while trying to run three thousand miles in record-breaking time.

He felt bad for Bruce. Frank wondered if the whole thing were his fault. Bruce had brought a lot to the table, and years later Frank spoke glowingly of the job Bruce had done organizing sponsorship details with United Way and working the PR machine along the route. He did the best he could, given the communication challenges. He made plenty of calls to outlets and left plenty of messages and did indeed make contacts, including bringing aboard Bogdan and Smith from the California College of Podiatric Medicine. And he helped get John a new bike when he desperately needed one. But without the conveniences of technology and at the mercy of Sonny's decisions behind the wheel, Bruce often failed to firm up promo opportunities.

"I defended Bruce in a big way," Frank said. "My father felt (Bruce) was sabotaging the run."

John was less sympathetic. "He talked about himself and what he wanted to do," John said. "He didn't reinforce anything about why he was there. He wasn't a participant. He was all about himself. To him, Dad was the driver and Ja was the cook."

Bruce would adamantly dispute John's version of events. "What he said simply wasn't true."

While the rest of the family was relieved over Bruce's departure, Frank felt the drumbeat of two familiar emotions: hurt and confusion. He had made another hasty decision in bringing Bruce aboard. They barely knew each other when they crossed paths that day in late July, just more than a month before the start of the run. Bringing Bruce in was a typical impulsive move by Frank, the gregarious short-sighted pleaser. He viewed the addition of Bruce as a convenient necessity. Yet in reality, Frank was inviting a relative stranger to a six-week, stress-filled road trip with the Gianninos. And Frank was doing it without even consulting family members, never mind considering the potential for conflict.

There was another pressing issue. "He was expecting money," Frank said. "I had promised him proceeds if there was any money. But the money was so small. I thought there would be more coming in, but it never materialized."

Sonny was well-versed in keeping his son's feet working properly with pseudo-surgery on his toenails and cuticles. Sonny was a pro in keeping his son loose and comfortable with expert massage. But he didn't know squat about public relations. And it showed. Frank largely blamed his dad for Bruce's departure, and the relationship between son and father grew tense.

"He and I butted heads quite a bit," Frank said. "After Bruce left, the PR fell off. We went days when nobody knew we were out there. I knew how important it was to have a constant flow of communication to the media and sponsors. You need to be recognized for what you're doing.

Eventually, though, "Dad figured out how to talk to the media. He got into the routine of being Bruce. But he was never as good as Bruce. I realized for the first time in my life that Dad wasn't perfect."

Back on the roads, Ja opened her diary.

Oct. 1: Day 31 -- Iowa (to just East of Des Moines),
4 a.m.-8 p.m.
70 miles

Well, another month is starting and about 18 days more to go. We were up and the same routine, farina, juice and they are off and running. Frankie's feet are coming along good. He might not lose the other nail. John is doing OK on the bike. His legs get stiff at times. He called his friend Joe the other night and got the latest news about school and friends.

We had a beautiful sunrise this morning. We are parked by a farmhouse. The children came out to wait for their school bus. They are all excited about us parked in front of their house. We are off again. We stopped in Stewarts to do the laundry. We had to turn off the highway. It was a nice Laundromat. The woman attendant was there. I loaded the machines and went to the motor home to start breakfast. I had the bacon and toast made. I went back into the Laundromat and Sonny went down the road to pick up Frankie and John. He came back and said he did not see them. I was almost finished. We got the clothes in the motor home and we were off to pick them up. We drove two miles up the road and Sonny thought they had not gone that far. So we backtracked and waited, still no Frankie and John.

So Sonny and Bruce had a disagreement. Sonny said they could not have gone that far and Bruce said his calculation said they did. Sonny was ready to punch him out. This moment had been brewing for a long time. This argument was going on while Sonny was driving. So back once more we go to Stewarts. We stopped at a store and Bruce asked if they had seen Frankie and John. The woman said she had seen them go by between 9:30 and 9:45, so we were off again to find them. We drove and they were waiting for us at the I-80 intersection.

So I finished breakfast and they ate. Frankie was going to run on I-80 for five miles, so we could pick up Route 90 that would take us into Des Moines. John did not ride on the Interstate. We got off at the exit four miles up the road. We saw Frankie coming. Someone was running with him. The man's family was traveling. He is a runner so he got out of the car and started running with Frankie. Frankie had to change the right shoe because it was bothering him. He ran the other mile on the Interstate to the next exit which took us to Route 90. We were on our way to Des Moines.

Bruce has not been feeling good for some time now. He is paranoid he really has a medical problem. When lunch time came around, he told Frankie he was going to leave to go home. He was not going to put up with another 16 days like today. We were glad he left. He was really beginning to irritate everyone with his attitude. The United Way people did not like his attitude either. After lunch we were met by the United Way. We received a police escort and everyone on the route was waving to us and blew their horns as we drove by. He was also met by some runners who ran with him.

We met Mayor Peter Crivaro in a downtown City square along with the people from the United Way. The mayor is Italian. He gave Frankie the key to the City of Des Moines. He is a very proud Italian. If we had time, he had planned to take us to his home for an Italian cooked meal. The TV stations followed us on the route to the square. When he gave Frankie the key to the city, he asked Frankie to sign it. He was planning to hang it in his mayor's office. He said he would take a picture of he and Frankie holding it and that he would mail the picture to Frankie. Sonny took pictures also. He is going to make a frame for it. He is a wonderful person. He showed us his appointment book and all the guest speaker appointments he has. He's going to speak at a Columbus Day affair and he will be talking about Frankie when he gives his speech. We gave him a press release about Frankie.

The police escorted us to the city limit. The sheriff then picked up escorting us. They led us another two miles into Altoona. Then the sheriff led us to a campground called Adventure Land. It was a beautiful place. They had a pool, lake, amusement park from what we could see at 9:00 o'clock at night. The office there was closed. They did not have any cards to register us so we parked for free.

I had supper all made, we ate, showered at the campground and went to bed.

11

Surprise Visitor

Frank's childhood was littered with embarrassments. He was one of the last of his buddies to learn how babies were made. His first schoolgirl crush, Joanne Skrainer in third grade, had a demoralizing twist. He was dancing with her while rehearsing for the musical "Oklahoma" when Frank tripped on her foot and fell.

One of his most vivid early memories of Catholic school at St. Catherine's in Blauvelt is of his fellow first-grade classmates making fun of specks of hair that grew on a birthmark at Frank's Adam's Apple. He already was insecure about his looks when, he said, a nun named Sister Bernadette yanked on the bulge in his throat.

In a fourth-grade gym class, Frank went to make a play in basketball when his head squarely met the face of another nun, Sister Gloria, bloodying her nose. Later, he earned a good old-fashioned soap-chewing punishment after dropping an F-bomb in class.

Other punishments included the single paddle, double paddle and triple paddle to his butt. Frank, a man of extremes, once got to feel the dreaded triple paddle after again spouting the F-word.

He tried to combat his insecurities with a flair for adventure. Frank loved being in the woods for their natural beauty and unlimited potential for self-discovery. He would take off his socks and shoes and catch turtles in a swamp near home. He loved a view, loved getting to the top, loved the smells of the woods.

Frank joined the Cub Scouts at age seven. At sixteen, he earned the rank of Eagle Scout.

The Scouts brought out Frank's leadership qualities and desire to give back to the community. He promised the Eagle Scout board that he would commit himself to volunteerism for the rest of his life. But even his success as a Scout failed to squelch his inner uncertainty. To Frank, becoming an Eagle Scout was more an endurance test, as running would become, than possessing any special quality.

"So you know what I did?" Frank said of his decision after receiving the Eagle Scout award. "I stopped."

There was no stopping now. The crew got a police escort into Des Moines to meet Mayor Crivaro, who invited the Gianninos to dinner. But Frank's legs were starting to tighten and Sonny explained that they must keep moving. Every minute was precious. Crivaro understood. But he wanted to thank Frank for his efforts.

So Crivaro handed Frank a key to the city – not exactly your typical key. This one was made of Styrofoam. Crivaro explained that he wanted to present a wooden key but didn't have time to get it prepared. They exchanged pleasantries and the crew went on their way.

The Gianninos discussed Bruce's departure at day's end. Frank thought his dad could have handled things better. But Frank clearly represented a minority of one in defending Bruce. Sonny reiterated his promise to leave if Bruce had stayed.

"No dad, that isn't the solution," Frank said. "We are a family. Family has to stick together."

"That's right, Son," Sonny said. "We are a family."

The family was soon out of Iowa and into Illinois, the seventh state in their journey. Frank was twenty-five miles into his morning run on a highway in Chicago Heights when a sports car pulled alongside him and John. A blond-haired figure stepped out of the car.

"Hey, are you that nut who's supposed to be running from San Francisco to New York?"

Frank instantly recognized the man and started laughing hysterically. It was Stan Cottrell, the world record-holder for fastest coast-to-coast run. Just three months earlier, he had set the mark by averaging 64½ miles for forty-eight days, totaling 3,103.5 miles from New York to San Francisco. Cottrell was joined by his doctor who was part of his support team for the record-breaking run.

Cottrell didn't show up for a social call, though he certainly possessed the gift of gab. Ever protective of his record, Cottrell rifled questions at Frank. Cottrell wanted to know about Frank's support team, his public relations methods, his routine, diet, physical issues. Everything.

No vitamins? What's that? Milkshakes? ... Milkshakes?

"So, what are you averaging now?" Cottrell asked.

"Seventy-plus," Frank said.

"Great."

Cottrell asked if he could run with Frank and join him for a day. A part of Cottrell might have wanted to share the running bond with a fellow adventure runner, and what better way than to join him side-by-side for a day. But the essence of Cottrell's appearance was clear, at least to Frank. Cottrell was checking up on his competition. The record-holder wanted to make sure the prospective record-breaker was following the rules.

"I'm on U.S. 30 and he jumps out of a sports car and starts running with me," Frank said. "He had his doctor friend with him. He asked him to drive ahead to the motor home and talk with my parents. I stop my running and we start talking. There was no negativity; he was there to check my legitimacy. I had told him a month before that I was shooting for sixty miles per day."

Frank ran a total of about seventy miles with Cottrell. At one point, Cottrell yanked Frank's arm deeper onto the shoulder as a speeding truck barely missed him.

"Thanks, Stan," Frank said. "I think you just saved my life."

Cottrell wasn't the only savior. Sonny had scored media coverage by alerting the Joliet United Way of Frank's arrival. A nearby newspaper met up with Frank. The reporter was in for some treat.

Frank and Cottrell met Joann Braam, a reporter for the *Herald News* in Joliet.

"Well," she said upon meeting Cottrell, "this story may turn out to be far more interesting than I planned."

"Well, it should, Ma'am," Cottrell said. "You have before you two of the most finely conditioned athletes in the country."

Frank looked quizzically at Cottrell, as if he was referring to someone else. *Two of the most finely conditioned athletes in the country?* Frank was hardly lacking in confidence by then. In fact, he was more confident about breaking Cottrell's record than about anything he had ever done.

But two of the most finely conditioned athletes in the country? The notion was hard for Frank to fathom.

"Actually, I wouldn't go quite that far Stan," Frank said. "My body isn't athletically designed."

"Of course we are finely conditioned and our bodies are athletically built," Stan said. "How else could we've run what we've run?"

Frank wasn't giving ground. Their runs were a matter of endurance, not athletic brilliance, he said. "At best, I know I am an average 10K runner or marathoner. Yeah, I can win a race once in a while, but I know my place as a competitor."

Stan talked about heading down to Kentucky to prove some things to ultra-marathoner associates. But Frank insisted on making the delineation between their exploits and those of, say, Bill Rodgers. That's when Frank hit on it, perhaps without realizing the full impact of his statement.

"Ours is more a matter of survival," he said finally.

Braam had run into a nice little story for herself. She asked Frank if his ability was based more on endurance than conditioning or natural athletic ability. "That's right," Frank said. "My body is not constructed for running. Shoes are hard on me. My feet are very narrow in the heel and very wide across the forefoot. Due to a skiing accident, one of my legs is about one-eighth inch shorter than the other, which throws my whole body out of balance."

Cottrell interjected. "Well, if that's your contention, Frank, how are you running seventy-mile days?"

Frank mentioned the orthotic work done by Bogdan and Smith from the California College of Podiatric Medicine. Frank didn't mention Bogdan and Smith's grim prognosis of Frank's zero percent chance of finishing the run because of those leg and foot issues.

The debate was in full swing between the world record holder and chaser. Cottrell reminded Frank that he wouldn't be able to continue day after day without being supremely conditioned – physically, mentally and emotionally. Braam, the reporter, wanted to know the mental and emotional preparation needed to attempt such a run.

"You need a lifetime of preparation, and when it comes to doing a run like this, everything has to click," Frank said. "My twenty-eight years of life experience are what prepared me for this. My passion for running led me to this. Now is the time when I can handle it all and savor it for the rest of my life.

"And thank God I have my family with me to do it. In my case, I didn't know if I could run all day, day after day. But before my first run, I had convinced quite a few people that I could do it. Then when I became a multi-day survivor of my first run, I knew I would do another, with plenty of support this time, to see how many miles I could pack in a day, day after day."

Frank invited Cottrell to run all the way to New York with him, but Stan declined. Cottrell stayed the night in the motor home with Frank and John while Ja and Sonny grabbed a hotel.

As Frank set out for his run the next morning, Cottrell asked what Frank was thinking.

"Nothing Stan," Frank said. "Nothing. Just want to get out there and run."

After breakfast, Cottrell called a sales rep for a ride, but the rep was fifteen miles away. As Frank headed into Indiana – his eighth state – Cottrell departed using another travel device of the times. He stuck out his thumb along the highway. Almost immediately, a car pulled up and Stan hopped in.

When he left, Frank was struck by the enormity of his run against a backdrop deep in silence. "Here we are running, and the only one who is monitoring me is Stan Cottrell," he thought.

Dad was no Bruce when it came to public relations. But one very influential individual was paying attention.

12

Frayed Nerves

Ruth Giannino was a stay-at-home mom who read a Harlequin Romance novel per day, enjoyed baking and owned a ceramic frog collection. Ruth wasn't nuts about converting to Catholicism. She tagged along to church miserably, but watched as the kids got their communions and confirmations.

Finances were a central issue in the family. The parents argued often, usually over funds, and Frank felt the sting of their battles. He loved his mom, who would later take a measure of biological credit for Frank's running success by citing her long legs. But he couldn't seem to satisfy her. He blamed her for the painful insecurity that developed from the first days he can remember.

"She would yell at me one moment and hug me the next," Frank remembers. "I believe she was depressed. She was loving most of the time. The big thing was, I wanted to make her happy all the time."

Ruth communicated well with most others. She got along nicely with Frank's girlfriends, remaining close to some of them even after the relationship ended with her son. But she had a communication void with the two oldest men in the house, both named Frank.

"I loved my mother unconditionally," Frank said. "She was my mom. But she had postpartum syndrome all the time I was growing up. A lot of what she said, I've blocked it out. I just remember the feeling of major insecurity."

To this day, Frank can't stand the sight of liver, a common blue-collar meal back in the 1950s, '60s and '70s. He hated the meal as a kid. Yet Ruth wouldn't let him leave the dinner table until he finished the course.

The root of Frank's issues was considerably more complicated than being forced to down liver. There were a lot of things going on at home, from the arguments to Frank's wounded self-esteem to a blanket of mystery enveloping the household.

Two Giannino babies died at birth, one before Frank was born, one after his birth. He believes they were both miscarriages. But to this day, Frank has no details about the deaths.

Not until 1991, at forty years of age, did Frank receive a telephone call telling him that oldest sister Marijean had been born out of wedlock. In fact, Marijean was in her forties when she learned of the circumstances surrounding her entrance into the world.

The medical profession opened Sonny's eyes to a lot of things, not least the price-gouging involved in medical care. He saw too many lives extended simply as a means for doctors and hospitals to profit from huge medical billing. And Frank's father had a great capacity for bluntness.

"Frank," Dad would tell his son, "we have weak hearts in this family. The men don't live very long."

Frank pooh-poohed Dad's flaws straight into adulthood. "He never believed in corporal punishment," Frank said. "He didn't even raise his voice. We could talk about anything. He was that voice at the other end of the phone all the time."

"He held a lot in – so did my mother," Frank's sister Nancy said. Nancy said her mom had an edge to her. "Dad, on the other hand, was affectionate with all of us."

His affection for Frank's run across America, however, had begun to wane.

Frank was reminded of his place in the cross-country pecking order every step he took. He thought little of his AAU shoes, which retailed for $22. But Frank had no bargaining position without another major sponsor stepping forward to foot the bill.

In fact, halfway through the run, Frank had his friend Bobby Bright ship him some New Balance 320s. But Frank wasn't keen on breaching his loyalty to – and contract with – AAU. He claimed later that he wound up barely wearing the New Balances.

The AAU shoes were tight, leaving the areas above the ankles, and at the shins, especially sore. "Every day my dad would stretch them out," Frank said.

But the shoe's stiffness had an underrated benefit by actually helping stabilize Frank's lower half.

In fact, Richard Bogdan, an instructor in the biomechanics department at California College of Podiatric Medicine who had met Frank before the run (and predicted Frank wouldn't finish) later drew another conclusion. The inflexible shoes were crucial to keeping Frank on the road.

Still, the pain was almost unbearable at times. Frank and his dad did everything possible to alleviate the hurt. Shoe Goo, moleskin, you name it and the Gianninos were using it to cushion the blow of six million foot strikes. Frank swore by compression socks, the specialized hosiery with a strong elastic. They helped increase blood circulation and force circulating blood through more narrow channels, thus causing more blood to return to the heart and less blood to pool in the feet.

Frank had learned another method to ease shin pain from one of his high school coaches, Bob Decker, who would use a thin roll of foam to separate the shin muscle from the shin bone, tape it up and apply the compression socks over it.

But there was only so much tinkering possible to decrease the pounding of three thousand miles. If Frank's howling feet weren't enough, the cranky motor home had been without hot water since the heater broke off. Near South Bend, Indiana, only ten days from the finish, Frank had a sponge bath. It was his first night on the trip without a shower or bath.

As they reached the Ohio border – the ninth state – Frank started to daydream. He suddenly remembered building box cars from scratch with his dad as a nine-year-old for the Cub Scout troop competition. The car would lose twice, but it didn't matter. It was an especially warm bonding experience with Dad.

Frank needed to revive those pleasant memories as tension grew with his father. Their stress began to mount in Tiffin, Ohio, with a week left in the run. The town had a large-scale running club, but a lack of notice from Sonny left Frank running solo through the area.

When he asked his dad about making contact with the United Way or the media, Sonny grew agitated. "Frank, you just don't realize the amount of pressure this thing has put on Ja and me," he said. "Sometimes I wonder if you truly care."

When Frank reminded his dad that these pressures were discussed before the trip, Sonny continued. "But here's what's bugging me. There's a little too much 'me, me, me' coming from you. We are doing this for you. Ja and I have worked harder than we've ever had to, and we haven't complained. You're obsessed with recognition from the media. There is a lot more to all of this than getting your picture taken."

"Dad, I know you and Ja are working hard, and I appreciate it."

"Then show it, Frank," Sonny said. "I am doing four jobs now – driving, map reading, maintaining this poor excuse for a motor home and taking care of your needs – and you are worried you're not getting your picture taken enough!"

The pressure and weariness started to engulf Frank and his dad. Frank was beyond burned out. He was emotionally, mentally and physically spent. Frank could have used a pick-me-up in Tiffin in the worst way – something, anything, to redirect his focus and shed the distracting issues with his father.

Team-wide exhaustion had left everyone on edge. Ja was so tired that she tried to pull panty hose over her slacks one morning. Sonny felt the dual pressure of trying to get himself and his son to the finish line. John, the Iron Man, was trying to hang on. Then there was Frank trying to refocus and bang out seventy-mile days.

Sonny's emotions went from anger to concern for his son. Sonny saw Frank tiring mentally. Frank's strength of mind had allowed him to clear repeated physical hurdles. But he was as good as finished if his mental framework started to weaken. Deep in football country, not far from where Knute Rockne employed his motivational genius at Notre Dame, Sonny Giannino began to crack the whip on his son.

Frank hit the road, recounting the conversation. He felt bad about being at odds with his dad. Jeez, he hoped he had expressed the proper appreciation to Ja and Dad for all they were doing. The more Frank thought about it, the more he understood the real source of Dad's ire. For once, Sonny was no longer the central figure, no longer the boss. He finally had grown weary of playing background vocals to Frank's cross-country dance. In retrospect, Frank thought, the scenario was inevitable.

Frank and John made their way into a Youngstown suburb called Boardman, near the Pennsylvania border. As they passed a workout gym, a man suddenly came out the gym door and ran almost smack dab into Frank. The man was heading out for his daily five-mile run.

"My name's Pat Perry," he announced.

"Nice to meet you, Pat," Frank said.

Little did Pat know that, by the time he left Frank that day, his life would never be the same.

13

The Run of His Life

Pat Perry was with his girlfriend and her friend driving on Route 224 and Youngstown/Boardman Road. They were going to work out at a fitness club when they spotted Frank and his motor home with the big sign, "Coast to Coast with AAU Shoes." They pulled into the parking lot of the club about one hundred yards ahead of the Giannino crew. Perry stepped inside the club and stood in front of a window watching the motor home.

"I was fixated, just staring at him," Perry said. "Whatever he was involved in, you could almost feel. I could feel some kind of energy and I didn't want to interfere with that."

So Perry continued to watch, mesmerized, while Frank started to run again. Perry's girlfriend, Sandy Lacivita, finally nudged him to go meet this guy going coast to coast. She knew that Perry needed to get closer, knew he would feel some form of regret if he didn't join the run.

Perry, twenty-seven at the time – a year younger than Frank – had run one marathon. He had focused on the science of the sport to offset a modest skill set growing up. Perry devoured *Runner's World* magazine. He studied running products and biomechanics. In the months before meeting Frank, Perry was cutting meat and doing wedding photography on weekends when he wasn't hanging out at the local Athlete's Foot store in the mall and turning down job offers from its manager, guy named Terry Apple, because of his hectic schedule that included a full college course load. Perry finally said 'yes' on the third offer, working a couple days a week. He was store manager within six months when Apple took a position at the company's headquarters in Pittsburgh.

In fact, Perry had met Stan Cottrell at a trade show and heard about alleged gaps in Cottrell's record-setting claim. But Perry didn't know the identity of the guy chasing Cottrell. Perry headed out the gym door to greet Frank.

But why? What made Perry take that final leap that would ultimately change his entire being, and not always for the better? What pulled him toward Frank instead of joining the thousands, maybe millions, of people who had seen Frank along the route without giving his run much more than a passing thought, if not a figurative middle finger?

Pat Perry wouldn't learn the answer to that question until years later. All he knew now was that he wanted what Frank had. Perry didn't know what Frank had, didn't know anything about him. Perry just sensed something special unfolding in front of him, sensed the thin guy with thick hair had something deep to offer.

"Do you mind if I stay with you?" he asked Frank.

Mind? Frank loved getting company on the road, loved breaking up runs with chatter, anything to temporarily steal his mind from the excruciating pain. And Perry's deep interest in the sport was blissful harmony. He was doing what Frank wanted to do by making a living out of running. Perry knew his stuff, for sure, but was fascinated by Frank's running knowledge. Frank enlightened Perry on details of his running success, like wearing sunglasses to prevent squinting, which kept facial muscles from tightening and leading to discomforts in other parts of the body such as the back of the neck, even the spine. Like leaning forward on downhills, not backward as Perry did, to keep from potentially landing stiff-legged and shocking the joints.

Perry's mind raced. He had never run farther than the 26.2-mile marathon standard. Now this stranger, this guy, this ... brother, was pulling him along like a guide dog, mile after mile after mile, subconsciously detailing the pain and the passion and the courage necessary for chasing dreams.

Frank, left, with Pat Perry, 1980.

"When I was running with Frank," Perry said, "he was gently trying to tell me what he was experiencing. Where he was, was a way different place. For some people, you can explain the challenge until you are blue in the face. You can show picture upon picture upon picture, but they'll never get it. I think for me, Frank showed me where the door was and gave me the key, and it was up to me to go through the door."

Perry joined the Gianninos for a breakfast break. He ran back to the gym to take care of business but promised to return. Twelve miles later, Pat was back with Sandy and her friend. They took pictures of Pat and Frank before the runners carried on.

Pat studied Frank the way he dug into running magazines and the latest shoe trends. At one point, Frank stopped and sat against an ice-cold guardrail, his eyes sunken, his body thoroughly drained. "You have no idea how much this hurts," Frank told Perry, who pointed out that he could only imagine the extent of Frank's pain darting up and down his body – dull aches, sharp aches, hospital-bed fatigue.

Oh yeah, there was pain everywhere. But at this moment, leaning up against the guardrail, Frank told Pat that his ass, which by this time had very little meat on it, was hurting more than anything.

"I remember we were running and at one point, he was running on a line and we brushed elbows a little bit," Perry said. "I barely touched him and he went off the berm and into the gravel. He was so finely balanced that the slightest little brush knocked him off his balance."

Youngstown had a running club with more than two thousand members. Perry told Frank how he would have had all kinds of runners along for the ride had he known of the run. But for once Frank needed no such attention and support. They needed only each other, and by the end of the day, Frank had set a one-day personal record by clocking 73.4 miles.

Pat Perry, never beyond the 26.2-mile wall, had run forty-three miles of them.

"He just kept running with me," Frank said.

A month later, Pat ran his first ultra race, a fifty-miler in Toledo, Ohio. He saw a story in *Sports Illustrated* about the Hawaii Ironman, the ultimate triathlon test consisting of a 2.4-mile swim, 112-mile bike and 26.2-mile run. Perry completed the Ironman in 1982, then did it again in '83. He ran two more ultra-marathons and also paced two friends, Cherry Stockton and Treacy McCamey, in separate Western States 100-Mile Endurance Runs in California.

Meantime, his career soared. He became a regional manager for Athlete's Foot. By '82, he was director of franchise services in which he trained owners to operate stores. Athlete's Foot was sold, yet Perry continued climbing the corporate ladder like Frank hammering through the Rockies, one step at a time, leading employees the way Frank had led him through his running limits, moving with the job from Pittsburgh to New York to California.

Perry was married in 1985 to a woman who was an Athlete's Foot employee when they met. They moved to Perry's roots in Youngstown, Ohio, and he continued going non-stop – training, working, training, working, training, working. He was prepping hard for a 508-mile bicycle race called The Great American Bike Race in California, one of the toughest ultra-cycling events in the world.

Perry had his crew in place, the minivan shadowing the rider and the motor home for the crew. All he needed was his wife. The Sunday before the race he called home to check on her arrival plans. Instead, he received a different itinerary.

"I'm not coming, and I want a divorce."

Perry never saw it coming. How could he? He was too busy working sixty hours a week and training another forty. His Saturdays consisted of one hundred and fifty-mile bike rides from five a.m. to five p.m. He did a two- to four-hour trail run on Sundays and headed for the pool if his body allowed. Sometimes it's hard to see the force from behind when you are always looking ahead.

"If you'd have asked me then, I wouldn't say I was a workaholic," Perry said. "I'd say I was Type A. At the time, I thought that is what it took to get the job done. But I was a workaholic. After twenty-two years and eighteen thousand hours of therapy, it's crystal clear."

Perry was an emotional wreck. He couldn't do the race. He couldn't do much of anything, including sleep. He took a flight home on Monday, drove back to California on Tuesday. Now it was Thursday and Perry hadn't slept in five days, his anxiety through the ceiling.

"Now I know what people mean when you hit rock bottom," Perry told his buddy Tony Clark. His friend replied rather strongly that, sorry pal, you are nowhere near rock bottom. Perry drove back to Ohio on Friday, non-stop in forty-four hours, fifteen minutes, still without a wink, and wouldn't work again for two years while in the throes of depression.

The divorce was finalized in January 1990. It was 4:32 p.m. the previous New Year's Eve when Perry sat on his couch and decided he wasn't moving until he stenciled a road map of his future. He wasn't moving – not to go to the bathroom, not to eat or drink – and he remained on the couch until 4:11 p.m. New Year's Day 1990.

He would go to California to visit friends and get some answers about this depressed, anxious guy on the couch. The problem with self-discovery, though, is that you don't always like the reflection.

Perry was outside a Mexican restaurant in Southern California with Clark watching a big orange sun touch the Pacific Ocean. It had been a year since Clark dismissed Perry's self-assessment on bottoming out.

"How did you know I wasn't at rock bottom?" he asked.

"You are still here," Clark said, "aren't you?"

Perry realized that rock bottom was when the heart took its last beat. Pat Perry was starting to understand why he had joined Frank on his run. It was like after his first Ironman, when folks asked if there was a time during the race when he wanted to quit. Actually there were several times Perry wanted to quit, he said, when the body and mind started their fascinating game play.

You reach a point when your body is done, depleted, finished, but your mind is still sharp and tells you, Perry's words, "Bullshit, come on. All the sacrifices you made and all the sacrifices family and friends made, you selfish bastard, and now you are going to quit because you are tired?"

"Then there comes the point when you are mentally shot and your body says to your brain, 'Jerkwad, you told me to do this. You get back in the game.'

"Somewhere down the road, your mind and body agree that you are done. At that point, you go to a place that you didn't even know you had, and you keep going.

"That was a place I didn't even know existed as I was staring at Frank. I had no frame of reference. But what I wanted, he had. I didn't know what that was, but he had it and I wanted it."

Perry's phone had a familiar ring once a month, like clockwork, during those two years. It was Terry Apple, the former Athlete's Foot manager who had given Perry his first job in the field.

"You ready to go to work yet?"

"Not yet."

"You ready to go to work yet?"

"Not yet."

"You ready to go back to work yet?"

"I think I am."

Apple got Perry a job with Asics, its headquarters a half-hour from Perry's residence in Huntington Beach, to put together a division of tech representatives. Perry hired nine tech reps and returned to working hard, training hard, playing hard, and was soon promoted to managing the company's national running line. He made a lot of changes within the conservative company and pissed off his share of people, until the late 1990s when a knock came on his office door from the company president.

"You spent eight hours yesterday deciding what type of shoelaces go into shoes," the president noted.

It finally dawned on Perry. He was gently being asked to leave.

One step forward, one step back. It was as if Perry had joined Frank all the way across America and they were still hammering miles. Perry bounced around the running shoe business, opening and operating two New Balance stores for six years in

Washington D.C., back to the West Coast but stopping in Ohio on the way.

Oh no, Perry's mom was having a reoccurrence of cancer. He wound up taking care of her for fifteen months until her passing at age seventy-six.

Perry reached California exhausted and unemployed. He hooked on with a company called American Sporting Goods to oversee its outdoor brand. In October 2013, Perry aligned with an old friend who started 361° USA and got it up and running in 2014.

"What that experience taught me was, Frank was my first teacher," he said. "In terms of the breadth and depth of what you are capable of, you don't know until you test yourself. If I didn't run to Frank, none of that would have happened."

He was referring to the good stuff – digging past barriers on the roads and taking his body to places it had never been. But those lessons that day with Frank gave Perry a starting point on his long road to self-awareness and self-discovery. Perry eventually realized that he had to navigate a deep forest of issues to reach an open valley of possibility.

But here's the thing. Perry impacted Frank almost as deeply. Perry gave Frank clarity and a sense of purpose not only years later, an eternal gift, but during the run, through the excruciating home stretch toward New York.

14

I Want to Quit

Not even the power of Perry could solve Frank's struggles, though, as he approached Pennsylvania. Frank was trying to endure what he would call an "emotional breakdown." None of his six pairs of shoes were holding up. His legs tattered, he resorted to soaking his feet in the motor home during twenty-five-minute breaks, which further incensed his father, mindful of the harm such soakings had done earlier in the trip.

Crossing into Pennsylvania, about four hundred miles from the finish line, presented the gang with all kinds of emotions. They were elated to be merely two states from the finish line. Yet they also knew the immense challenges that Pennsylvania presented. Running through Pennsylvania would be a bear thanks to its mountainous rolling-hills terrain and rural setting filled with winding, shoulder-less roads causing safety hazards. Just as concerning, the route lacked convenient facilities to allow constant water in the motor home. Water deficiencies affected almost every integral part of the mission, from drinking to cooking to showering and, of course, to running.

The crew got an immediate break on the longest day of the run. In their quest for fresh water, Sonny and Ja struck up a conversation with a grocery store owner. The store owner smiled when asked about the location of fresh water. He led the Gianninos to his farm and offered up, as the man put it, "the sweetest water in these parts."

But the quest had just begun. Cars and trucks sped past within inches of Frank and John. Sonny squashed the usual procedure of driving ahead for three-mile intervals, instead creeping behind the brothers with the motor home lights flashing. Frank and John almost blindly navigated the treacherous roads, desperately trying to prevent a bad step or wrong pedal push that could lead to injury and jeopardize the entire run.

Frank was busting out the miles. There were no bathroom facilities to be found, so Frank dropped a deuce in a roadside sewer drain, hardly his first intimate brush with nature. The family met up with a United Way official later in the day, and media awaited at State College, home of Penn State University. By now the questions were redundant, the answers polished. Frank went into a dissertation about seeing the world and each day experiencing a new and temporary home, about how he would savor the experiences for the rest of his life. Frank was flying high, ready to motor straight out of the Quaker State and into New Jersey. Then it was home free, the world record his, a lifetime of accomplishment at age twenty-eight.

One step forward …

One step back.

Frank was dragging ass by the third full day in Pennsylvania. Of course it wasn't his first dip into the emptiness of exhaustion. But this was a special type of weariness. Old calluses on his feet had softened to become open sores thanks to Frank's brilliant idea – yet again – of soaking his feet between runs. Frank was in awful pain. He hobbled. He didn't want to run another step. Worse, he didn't think he *could* run another step.

Every single stride required all the energy he could muster. *Six million steps.*

Frank started to walk. Then he stopped.

Reaching New York suddenly and dramatically felt like a low priority. He fantasized about finishing up his run across America inside the motor home.

"I'm tired, John," Frank told his little brother, voice lowering, "really tired."

John tried to lighten the mood. "Why should you be tired, Frankie. You've only been running almost seventy miles a day for forty-three days. You have no reason to be tired."

John's humor was lost on Frank. He was almost in tears.

Frank finally had come eyeball to eyeball with his greatest fear, the greatest fear of all athletes, really. "I want to quit, John. I really want to quit. For the first time, I just want to sit down and never move again. I'm frustrated. I'm fighting depression. I've been pushing through pain every day."

"But there are only three days left to run," John said hopefully. "What about the record?"

Frank was reduced to a whisper. "Who cares?" he said. "I am so tired of all this."

***

As a kid, Frank had grown accustomed to being left behind, only now it involved his friends going off to four-year colleges. Frank hadn't even bothered applying to a single four-year school. His parents couldn't really afford it, for one. And Frank hardly was prepared for the transition.

"Frank, I'll give you $1,000 for college if you need help," his dad offered.

Frank didn't think he was up to it anyway. He was only running a shade under 10:00 for two miles, so there were no scholarship offers. He also lacked the confidence to jump right into a four-year school.

So he enrolled at Orange County Community College (OCCC), a junior college a couple towns over in Middletown, New York. Frank figured to pursue a teaching degree in mathematics. He liked math because he could figure it out. There was, for the most part, a clear-cut beginning and ending to math, unlike so many of his thoughts. And teaching would be a natural extension of his personality and interest in helping others.

But Frank's real passion was running. College was what he was supposed to do. Running was what he loved to do. He ran local races. He enjoyed the running lifestyle, aptly described as logging mucho miles and living on impulse and a shoestring budget.

Frank treated college as another adventure. He and buddy John Santacroce barely had fifty dollars between them when they strapped on backpacks and hitchhiked to Florida for spring break freshman year. They headed straight for the ocean upon arriving at Daytona Beach, threw down their packs and jumped into the water. They met some girls from Michigan and wound up staying two weeks.

Frank was nineteen and working three full-time jobs – at a music shop, pumping gas and on a village beautification project in his hometown – during his sophomore year in '71. But somebody else had a plan for Frank. Not his mom or dad, but an uncle – Uncle Sam.

The military draft was in full swing as the Vietnam War raged. Frank had received a relatively low number in the lottery that summer, twenty-nine, meaning a high probability of getting drafted. He had no interest in shooting anyone, and especially no interest in dodging bullets. But Frank felt a patriotic duty to the country and to his dad, a proud Army veteran. Frank met a schoolmate at OCCC who had managed to steer clear of gunfire as an Army clerk. Frank decided that he wanted to be an Army clerk.

Most of his friends were less gung-ho about joining the military. One became a conscientious objector. Frank's buddies were hardly alone. In January 1972, Frank noticed three-quarters of the folks on his bus headed to New York City's Whitehall Street were drunk, stoned or tripping on acid in desperate attempts to fail their physical.

Frank tried to control his own fate in the Army by enlisting, which essentially lowered his chances of being placed in combat. Having been granted a delayed enlistment so he could get his associate's degree, Frank left for basic training at Fort Dix, New Jersey, in June 1972.

"I was in it to get out," Frank said. "I looked at the military as an obligation."

Ruth Giannino had the same feelings many moms and dads had during the time. She thought her boy was going off to die. As Frank pulled out of his family's home for Fort Dix, Ruth stood in the full glass storm door of their Walden home crying. It was a scene played out across America, whisker-stubbled kids barely old enough to legally down a beer heading off to shoot the Viet Cong before returning home in body bags.

Frank didn't think about dying. But how could he be so sure of being spared? He already had witnessed the perils of war up close as a teen when neighbor Ray DeMeola briefly returned from the Army wounded, crying his eyes out to a pastor in his living room.

"Don't let me go back! I'm going to die!"

DeMeola was sent back to war, and a month later, on May 14, 1969, he was dead at the age of twenty-one.

Frank got an early taste of what he hoped to avoid in the Army. His lasting scene from Fort Dix was an exercise called "Escape and Evasion," in which Frank's two hundred and fifty-strong battalion tried to avoid being "captured" by the enemy. Those caught would be taken to a mock POW camp for interrogations. As he walked along a road with a handful of soldiers, flares darted in the sky above and Frank suddenly ran into the woods.

"The minute I saw trouble, I ran," Frank said. "I wound up on a road after running five miles through the woods mostly alone. I just don't think I would have handled combat. I think I would have been killed just like Ray."

Frank got lucky when the Army accommodated him with a series of desk jobs. He was a clerk/typist on the clock from 7:30 a.m. to 2 p.m. Frank was thrilled to be the low man on the totem pole. It allowed him to perform his menial tasks and spend free hours honing his running skills. Frank did his own running workouts at Fort Dix, happily burning mile after mile in Army boots. If you are a runner, Frank liked to say, the focus of almost every day is your run. He so looked forward to daily five- to six-mile jaunts. And when Frank heard the one-mile base record was four minutes, fifty-five seconds on the track, he ran it in 4:51 in those combat boots, lapping the other forty-nine members of his platoon before they lifted him on their shoulders in celebration. The Army was doing wonders for Frank's running.

He was at Fort Huachuca in Sierra Vista, Arizona, for advanced basic training when he tuned in to the '72 Olympic

Marathon. Frank was a diehard Steve Prefontaine fan, loving his cojones and toughness, his balls-out approach to everything he did, especially in the confines of a foot race. Frank wished he had possessed the same approach, but even those occasions when he discovered his intestinal fortitude, Frank usually lost precious energy through nerves, and he'd ended up fading in the end. Not Pre.

Frank idolized Pre, just a year older, despite the '72 marathon champ, Frank Shorter, having grown up a few towns over from Walden in Middletown. "My junior year of high school, Pre exploded onto the scene," Frank said. "He ran a mile in 4:03.6 his senior year in high school in '69. He was doing things other guys weren't doing. He was a smaller guy, wasn't a pretty runner. He wasn't a gazelle – he was all guts. I was so inspired by him."

Frank was stationed in Arizona when he watched Shorter win the Olympic race. Two months later, on Nov. 2, 1972, Frank received orders to go to Vietnam. The cushy desk job was no longer complementing his running career.

Frank was being sent to war.

Then he got the biggest break of his life.

One hour after receiving his orders, they were canceled when President Nixon chose to pull troops out of Vietnam. Instead, in December 1972, Frank got another assignment – to beautiful Alaska, of all places.

He worked in an office from 7:30 a.m.-2 p.m., for agents doing background checks and other investigative procedures for the military. Frank again had an abundance of free time. He would jump into his VW van and take off for weekends. Frank replaced the passenger seat with a bed. He sampled a number of gorgeous mountain regions and spent the nights in the van. He ran local races and immersed himself in the running community. Frank almost always tackled the mountains, and came away from those workouts believing he could go almost any distance.

"I had it made up there," he said. "I did nothing."

Frank could run decently for long periods of time. But his long-distance potential remained untapped until he met a fellow runner, Captain John Blair. Captain Blair introduced Frank to high-velocity training that left him feeling and believing he could run, not only longer, but faster.

Blair was performing high-mileage training for the 1973 Boston Marathon in hope of breaking two hours, forty minutes, around a 6:00 per-mile pace. His training was highlighted by tempo runs, shorter workouts at race pace. The idea was to condition the body to handle a pace that would allow you to eventually run longer races, such as the marathon, at a fast rate.

In fact, Shorter had just won a gold medal by utilizing a surge near the nine-mile mark that incorporated tempo training. Shorter had built his training around six, 800-meter runs, the first and last 200s in thirty-five seconds and the middle 400 in sixty seconds. He credited the training with breaking away and dusting the field in Munich.

Frank Giannino had little experience with tempo runs when he set out to help Blair prepare for the famed 26.2-miler in Boston. Their training goal was to run ten miles in an hour. The 6:00 per-mile pace would produce an upper-echelon marathon time of 2:37:12. Frank had never finished a long-distance workout that fast. When he finally did it, Blair's words rang in Frank's head forever.

"You did it," Blair told Frank. "Now you have to keep that pace for a marathon. You have the ability. You can do it."

Frank knew he could handle a 6:00 pace for an entire marathon. Once he crossed that barrier, who knew what was next? A 5:45 pace? A 5:30 pace? Frank was on the cusp of a running breakthrough. But his life had become a series of breakthroughs and letdowns. One step forward, one step back. Dusting the neighborhood kids as a pre-teen, losing to the high school stars as a growing boy. Whirlwind romances, torturous breakups. Bubbly on the outside, pained on the inside.

And now this: A running epiphany followed by a skiing catastrophe.

Skiing?! What was Frank doing on a ski slope?!

It was the last week of February 1973 when Frank headed to Fort Richardson ski area near Anchorage to try his hand at skiing for the first time. Two weeks after breaking through with Blair,

Frank broke something else on the slopes. He was trying to figure it all out when a binding failed to release.

"I hit a series of small moguls," he remembered. "I was totally inexperienced and the right ski binding didn't release. My right knee bent at an odd angle."

Frank's medial collateral ligament and meniscus in the knee were all messed up. Healing and recovery were complicated by a lack of sophisticated arthroscopic procedures at the time. Surgery left Frank with his right leg one-eighth of an inch shorter than his left. The leg-length discrepancy would have long-term effects to the right side of his body, namely neck pain and soreness in his right arm while running long distances. He often experienced pain in his groin area, right hip, the lower right side of his back and the right side of his neck and shoulders – to name just a few sore spots.

Frank was only twenty years old. But the accident forced him to learn methods of pain management, including using proper shoes, socks and orthotics. The alternative was spending the rest of his running life in pain and discomfort.

"It wasn't that I was the most original guy," he said. "I'd copy others. I read a lot."

Frank made do with the skills he had. He won a fifteen-mile race and was one of the top finishers in the inaugural Mayor's Midnight Sun Marathon in 1974, both in Anchorage. Frank broke through in the '75 Maryland Marathon, finishing twenty-eighth with a time of 2:39:34, just more than a 6:00 per-mile pace.

Despite the accident, Frank's thirty-two months in Alaska were some of the most bittersweet moments of his life. He experienced the ultimate runner's high – navigating mountains, sucking in flawless air, clicking off miles while watching his times drop. This was running heaven. There was no telling how far and fast he could go.

Then a telegram arrived in the spring of '74. It was from his dad.

"Your mother's in critical condition. She may not live to the morning. Come home."

Huh?! Frank had received an audio letter from his family not long before the telegram. It was narrated by his dad and included his mom, sister Nancy and eleven-year-old brother John chiming in. Ruth sounded okay. "I'm in my usual recovery position, having a good day compared to the rest," Frank remembered his mom saying in the audio.

Ruth had been fighting cancer for nine years. She had a mastectomy and then another one. She wasn't feeling well, no doubt. But Frank thought she was managing her cancer. He had no idea the devil's disease had returned en force, that her entire spinal column was loaded with deadly cells. He had no idea she was about to die.

Frank was pissed at his father. How could he have failed to keep his son informed of Mom's declining health? Why must families be so secretive? Who does it really protect in the end?

Nancy remembered her dad writing letters to her sisters, who were living in California, detailing Ruth's sickness. But he never mailed them.

"I think he was in denial," Nancy said. "I remember hearing her tell my father, 'Find a good mother for John, and don't let them hook me up to machines.'" On one occasion, she pointed to a woman on a respirator and told her husband, "Don't let me look like her."

Now she was having a last-chance surgery and the odds were that she would die on the operating table. And Dad had chosen to break the news to Frank with a telegram?

Frank flew out that day and arrived at the hospital just after Ruth's surgery the following day. She lay in the recovery room on a respirator as Frank held her hand. He asked a nurse if his mom was aware of her surroundings.

"Absolutely," came the answer.

Frank suddenly felt a voluntary movement. "I love you, Mom," he said, bursting into tears.

She spent the next three weeks on the respirator. The family was together at home when the call came on March 19, 1974. Ruth Giannino was dead at the age of forty-nine.

"It was the only time I saw Dad break down, when he got that call that pronounced her dead," Frank said.

Frank inherited Ruth's long legs, and she liked to take credit for his running prowess. But while Ruth had outwardly supported Frank's running, she was able to make just that one high school meet. She didn't drive and was pretty busy around the house and often weakened by her cancer. Frank accepted that she couldn't make it out to see him run.

But now she would never see him lace up the running shoes again.

Death is strange. It can invade without warning or discrimination as the cruelest of passings – an accident or a sudden illness or the result of a bizarre undiagnosed condition. Or it can arrive at the end of a torturous, long-term illness like cancer, forcing loved ones to root for death over life, stopping over continuing.

Mourning can be even stranger. When the last heartbeat rips a hole in the hearts of those closest, there is no reactionary protocol. You make decisions on gut instinct, spouting clichés like "she would have wanted it that way" or "Mom is smiling down upon us."

Very often you don't know exactly how to act or feel. Sometimes you just try to find a comfortable place in the moment to delay the excruciating onset of painful mourning. Frank's feelings were especially hard to decipher given his complex relationship with Mom.

"I had a love-hate relationship with her," he said. "Her being overweight really bothered me."

The idea that Frank would point to weight as a factor in his relationship with Ruth might sound especially odd. But Frank's quirkiness extended to vanity. Just like Ruth's weight gain following the birth of her first child bothered Frank's father, so too did it bother Frank.

"I know I have buried a great deal of my past and what it was like to grow up with her as my mom," Frank said. "I have forgotten a lot of the words shared back then, but I do remember the way she made me feel at times. I was a pretty insecure kid, so I would solicit praise by looking for approval. I would say things to my mom like, 'Mom, aren't I the greatest?'

"But instead of realizing I was looking for support, she would tear me down. It was frustrating to me and I know it was the source of many of my insecurity issues. I believe my lifelong issue – the need to seek the approval of others – has had a great deal to do with my relationship with her."

Frank was discharged from the Army in June 1975. Once again, he had no real plan for what to do with his life. He knew only that he wanted to run and see the land. Frank spent his first summer out of the Army traveling before enrolling that fall at the State University of New York at New Paltz to finish his math degree.

He lasted two semesters studying math at SUNY New Paltz. He met the girl of his dreams during that time at school, Patty Whelan. He also found out what he didn't want to do with his life. He didn't want to become a math teacher.

Frank and Mike Leming, a buddy he had met in the Army, took a road trip to Montreal to see the 1976 Summer Olympics. Frank didn't have any money, of course, or event tickets. But that didn't stop him from searching out Olympic parties and reaching the entrance to Olympic Stadium to see Shorter, who was looking for his second straight Olympic marathon gold medal, as he entered the stadium behind Waldemar Cierpinski, the East German runner who later would be tied to a state-sponsored performance-enhancing drug program.

Just after the Olympics, Frank tried college again, this time with Patty at Northern Arizona University. He had decided to earn his graduate degree in parks and recreation management. Frank walked on to the cross country team and ran in a few meets. He could go five miles at 5:30 pace, but it wasn't good enough to make the Division I program's travel team. NAU's top seven runners traveled to meets. Frank was about the twentieth best runner on the team.

"Flagstaff was all about being in a beautiful place," he said. "What gave me the most joy was the workout, new trails. The other thing I loved was climbing to the top peak and looking down to get a snapshot of the community."

Frank couldn't compete at the top level, but he easily recited the numbers and names and schools associated with distance-running greatness. He was well-versed in the University of Oregon running empire developed by coaches Bill Bowerman and later Bill Dellinger, studying up on guys such as the great Alberto Salazar (three-time New York City Marathon winner) and Matt Centrowitz (an Olympian in 1976 and 1980) and Rudy Chapa (a six-time All-American, 1978 NCAA 5,000-meter champ), Bill McChesney (Oregon's 5,000/10,000 record-holder) and Don Clary (1984 Olympian), and of course Steve Prefontaine.

After being dumped by Patty, Frank wanted to experience the scene first-hand – he felt as though he needed to – and he enrolled at the University of Oregon to focus on therapeutic recreation with an eye toward working in a jail like his dad. On his first day in Eugene, Frank ran to the site of where Pre had died in a car crash two years earlier.

Frank was going to ride that adventurous streak of his until he figured out his ambitions in life. But he was plotting his future without knowing it. Frank was starting to open up, starting to feel more comfortable in his own skin. He strummed the guitar in front of dozens of fellow students, making good on those lessons Dad had purchased, after wrecking Frank's guitar, all those years earlier.

"I wanted something," he said. "But I didn't know what it was going to be. I ran every day, sometimes more than once."

He entered local road races. He set a 6.2-mile personal best of 32:59, a finish that said as much about Oregon's highbrow competition (good for just forty-first place) as it did for his maturing speed and endurance. Frank lasted five months at Oregon. His seminal moment came, not on the track or trails, but while working on a class project in a course called volunteer management. Frank's idea was to stage a "Bathtub Squeeze" contest with the goal of setting the Guinness Book of World Records in the event, assuming there was such a category.

Frank got a tub from a local landfill and sold the competition as a potentially record-breaking event. He got tons of pre-event publicity. Two television stations from Portland came down. Newspapers covered it. They came together to see a bunch of college kids given three minutes to squeeze into a six-foot tub anchored by two-by-fours set atop gym mats that cushioned potential falls.

On the day of the great bathtub squeeze-in being held in the Erb Memorial Union gym, the famous cafeteria scene from the movie *Animal House* was being filmed as well. But that didn't keep twenty-one teams from competing, with the winner shoehorning nineteen people into the tub and staying inside for the requisite twenty seconds.

Frank had managed and promoted his first major event. Nope, it wasn't perfect. And no, he didn't make the Guinness Book of World Records. He learned a valuable lesson about details when his grade came back a B-plus. What had cost him an A, said the professor, was failing to send out thank you notes to all the folks who had helped organize the event.

Frank was still without his graduate degree, but he knew one thing. He was finished with college. Frank was twenty-five years old. He was broke. He was homesick. It was time to return to Orange County, New York. Time to go home.

"I went to two of the most beautiful places on Earth," he said of Flagstaff and Eugene. "I realized that everything I was fond of – trail running, the running culture – made home the place I wanted to be. I really missed running up on the Gunks (the Shawangunk Mountains)."

Frank viewed life in the moment. He took a $300-a-week recreation job at a jail near home. That lasted six weeks when Frank got far too close to a stabbing and full-scale brawl during an inmate basketball game.

Now twenty-six, he became recreation director for a branch of AHRC, the Association for the Help of Retarded Children, near home. Frank and a co-worker set up activities for the special-needs population, taking them to the movies or shopping.

"I really had no desire other than to be a running bum," he said. "I wanted something. But I didn't know what."

He lived in a downstairs basement apartment in New Paltz and logged the heaviest mileage of his life. Frank and running buddies Billy Glatz and Bob Bright went on long runs – eight miles, fourteen miles, twenty miles – along picturesque roads and the world-renowned trails on the Shawangunk Mountains.

Billy would later help found a local club called the Shawangunk Runners Club, based in New Paltz. Frank grew close to both runners. They often broke up runs for a quick beer stop at a friend's home before finishing up.

Frank, Glatz and Bright headed to Massachusetts to run the 1978 Boston Marathon. The day before the race, Frank walked into Bill Rodgers' running store. Frank was wandering around the store when he came across the book that would change his life.

15

Runnin' My Life Away

Frank's dad pulled the motor home off to the side of the road. His temper had been brewing toward a boil for some time, ever since he chased away Bruce Goldberg. Now it was Frank's turn to get walloped by Sonny's explosion.

"You have to finish this for me and, especially, Ja and John," Sonny said. "We've all worked very hard to get to this point!"

Nobody had worked harder than Josephine Giacalone. Ja grew up in a middle-class family on Wright Avenue in Auburn, New York. She had two sisters, one older (Rose) and one younger (Cay), and a brother named Joe. Ja worked at General Electric and, like her sisters, appeared to be well on her way to the life of a single woman. She was schoolmates of both of Frank's parents, and the Giacalones and Gianninos were family friends through the years.

When Sonny's mom passed away a month after Ruth died in 1973, Ja attended the wake and got to talking with her old friend. They quickly realized how much they had in common, and only six months after Ruth's passing, Josephine and Sonny were married.

The union raised eyebrows among family members who thought Sonny had rushed into matrimony, breaking that unofficial one-year grace period following the death of a spouse. But Sonny wasn't one to follow the norm or political correctness. He felt comfortable around Ja, felt he could speak his mind without being judged or ridiculed. And Ja, by all accounts, was a marvelous catch.

Still, it was a difficult time for the Giannino kids. Frank's sister Nancy said Dad "went psycho" after Ruth died. He threw away all of her stuff. His fuse got shorter and he became unpredictable. So most of the Giannino children were overwhelmed when their dad met Ja. Sonny didn't just have to win over the Giacalone family, which he did convincingly. He had to win over his own family, not because of any faults of Ja, but because of his quick courtship following Ruth's death.

Resentment among Sonny and his older daughters was such that Marijean and Barbara, living in California, weren't invited to the wedding. But Ja went out of her way to make the transition as smooth as possible for everyone involved. The siblings soon embraced Ja, and certainly appreciated her positive influence on Dad.

"Ja can adapt to any atmosphere," Frank said. "She was one hundred percent loyal to Dad. I saw them debate and discuss, but I never saw them argue – not once."

She had her opinions like everybody else. But Ja was kind and compassionate and loyal. She was a terrific listener who studied people and situations before drawing conclusions. Frank described her as a chameleon because of her ability to adapt to all circumstances and surroundings, ideal qualities for the trip across America.

And of course Ja's spectacular work at the stove would help get her stepson on the road every bit as much as Sonny or John or the creaky motor home.

She did all the cooking and laundry and cleaning, determined to keep the motor home as spiffy as the home she shared with Frank's dad back in Walden. If there was a Guinness Book record for laundry done per minute, she would have set her own mark by doing eight loads in two hours, ten minutes late in the run.

In fact, Ja would insist later that despite Frank's dinner-table memory of his dad's brainstorm, it was her idea for the family to head the support team. Naturally it was done with Ja's endearing subtlety.

"I was the one who said to my husband, 'We might as well go with him,'" Ja said. "At least we know what to do for him." I wanted him to be most successful. And we met a lot of wonderful people along the way.

Ja probably had the second most difficult job on the trip. She had the sometimes challenging task of keeping her husband on an even keel, free from the emotional pitfalls of supporting, not just a transcontinental runner, but a son obsessed with realizing his goal. She was up first, anywhere from one-thirty a.m. to four a.m. every day, and sprang into action by preparing breakfast. That usually involved slapping together a cream of wheat-like dish with brown sugar they called Gookinaid.

"They woke me up and it was always ready," John Giannino said. "That was the great thing about Ja –everything was planned out. You sat down to eat and it was there. There was no wait. It was all based around Frankie – how he was feeling, what he wanted."

Or as Frank put it, "Dad made sure the family's home was environmentally safe. Ja made sure it was homey."

The meals weren't exactly a choice between peanut butter and tuna sandwiches. Ja's menu included elaborate offerings such as lasagna and chicken cacciatore, which might seem like a modest task until you factored her efforts inside a moving vehicle with various kitchen parts breaking down at a rate comparable to Frank's body. The scene was almost comical at times, with Ja trying to slice and dice and balance as Sonny took turns too fast or discovered potholes, at which point the kitchen door or oven crashed open with a temperamental thud.

"One thing about Ja, she was always there," John said. "She rarely complained. I wouldn't say she was easy-going. I would say she was accommodating. If you asked her opinion, she would give it to you. But she never forced it on anybody. She took care of me. Her morals were very old-fashioned. You would be nice to people. Cursing was out."

"I don't know where I got the energy," Ja said. "It was just continuous work."

She had a special humility essential to a successful voyage. There was room for just one big ego in the party – Frank's. He needed to possess an arrogance that would push him through three thousand miles of pain and discomfort. The success of the run depended largely upon the crew's unselfishness and determination toward helping the runner. Ja was the perfect fit in Frank's imperfect grind of maintaining heavy daily mileage.

Only now Frank needed more than Ja's tasty meals and motherly touch. He needed his dad's wake-up call. For the first time in the run, Frank had given into a deep lack of confidence, those familiar childhood feelings of doubt and insecurity charting their course once again. Frank was completely burned out.

"I was really frustrated, fighting depression," Frank said. "A lot of work had gone into it, and I was looking for the end."

An intensely bizarre, and largely inexplicable, part of running across the country was the sudden switch from agony to acceptance. The great ultra-marathoner Marshall Ulrich has used all kinds of devices to condition his mind to overcome seemingly unbearable pain. One memorable occasion in his own cross-America run years later was to disassociate himself from his right foot when plantar fasciitis and a tear in a tendon hobbled him about one-third of the way through the run. "This foot doesn't belong to me anymore," Ulrich announced. "It doesn't fit in with who I am, what I am trying to do or where I am going. This is not my foot."

In other cases, a runner's outlook could be suddenly lifted by a cheer from the crowd or a single smile-and-wave from a passerby, or a child's adoring grin. Or, on this painstaking day in Pennsylvania, a simple song, a song that had become Frank's running mantra since departing San Francisco a month and a half earlier. Not surprisingly, the pick-me-up came from the unsung hero of the run, the seventeen-year-old Valley Central High senior delaying his final year of school to help his big brother break a record. John Giannino.

"John knew me like a book," Frank said.

John slipped a familiar cassette tape into the boom box – Eddie Rabbitt's just-released single, "Drivin' My Life Away," about a roadie and his long periods away from home. As usual,

Frank altered the lyrics by one word, "runnin'" instead of "drivin'."

Well the midnight headlight finds you on a rainy night
steep grade up ahead slow me down makin' no time
gotta' keep rollin'
those windshield wipers slappin' out a tempo
keepin' perfect rhythm with the song on the radio
gotta' keep rollin'
Ooh I'm RUNNIN' my life away, looking for a better way, for me
ooh I'm RUNNIN' my life away, looking for a sunny day
Well the truck stop cutie comin' on to me
tried to talk me into a ride said I wouldn't be sorry
but she was just a baby
Hey waitress pour me another cup of coffee
pop me down jack me up shoot me out flyin' down the highway
lookin' for the morning
Ooh I'm RUNNIN' my life away, looking for a better way, for me
ooh I'm RUNNIN' my life away, looking for a sunny day
Well the midnight headlight find you on a rainy night
steep grade up ahead slow me down makin' no time
gotta' keep rollin'
those windshield wipers slappin' out a tempo
keepin' perfect rhythm with the song on the radio
gotta' keep rollin'
Ooh I'm RUNNIN' my life away, looking for a better way, for me
ooh I'm RUNNIN' my life away, looking for a sunny day.

Dad's words were effective. There was no person Frank ever wanted to please more than his father. But the sound of the song and its lyrics were magical. Frank strengthened his resolve. He had only two hundred miles left, for crying out loud. He repeated the basics of running – one foot after another. Frank somehow discovered another gear.

"It's like me in business," Frank said. "I keep pushing and pushing and pushing. And finally, there's daylight."

He looked at John and smiled wide. Frank started to widen his stride length as well. He laughed. A light rain dripped onto the gorgeous countryside. Frank started running through Pennsylvania. In Danville, the high school cross country coach and his team unexpectedly joined Frank. They ran together for four miles.

Frank wasn't going to quit, not now, not ever. One step at a time. One mile at a time. One town at a time.

One day at a time.

He made it to Easton, Pennsylvania, on the evening of Day Forty-Five. He was on world-record pace with one day to go.

16

The First Finish Line

The biggest day of Frank Giannino's life started at 2:50 a.m. on Oct. 17, 1980. It was time to go break a record, time to make something of himself, something that would single him out for the rest of his days.

And he was flying high.

Frank smoothly broke into a sub-10:00 per-mile pace, at least a couple minutes quicker than usual, for the first twelve mostly downhill miles. In fact, Frank threw in at least one 8:00 mile – on the forty-sixth day of running! – that would have qualified as a pretty good 10K pace. Frank was sniffing the finish line. There was no stopping him now, his thick beard developed long ago from the burden of shaving. Frank crossed the Delaware River into New Jersey, the eleventh state.

An independent film producer named Joel Shapiro arrived on the scene a day earlier. He had been hired by Intermark, the company sponsoring Frank's run, to film the final two days as a promotional tool for the company's AAU Shoes line. Intermark president Joel Sedley showed up with James Cohan, vice president of the Cleveland-based Nelson Stern Advertising Agency, which handled advertising for Intermark. A newspaper reporter in Somerville, New Jersey, interviewed Frank.

Bogdan met up with Frank in the central New Jersey town of Dunellen. An Elizabeth, New Jersey, native, Bogdan was the California podiatric professor who had joined Chris Smith in concluding that Frank's legs weren't fit to go three thousand miles. But Bogdan and Smith had played key roles in making it happen, first as unintentional motivators, then as podiatric experts getting Frank into the correct orthotics. Bogdan joined Frank in running out of San Francisco. Now he was going to jog with him to the finish line.

There was time for one more wrong turn, always time for another wrong turn, this time in Plainfield, New Jersey. The runners quickly realized their mistake and headed into Elizabeth. They took a right off Route 28 onto Elmora Avenue. It was six p.m. and getting dark. Eight miles to go. The Goethals Bridge connecting Elizabeth to Staten Island was two miles away. Frank would finish at the toll booth on the Verrazano-Narrows Bridge, which connected Staten Island to Brooklyn – famous as the starting point for the New York City Marathon.

There would be a ceremonial finish the following day on the Brooklyn Bridge, giving sponsors time to unveil their conquering hero to the press. But the toll booth at the Verrazano-Narrows was the official finish, the time and location that would be measured for Guinness' world-record qualification.

There was one problem, however. One major problem. Pedestrian traffic wasn't allowed on the Goethals. It was the final result of poor planning and a dearth of available information on roads and bridges. Even if Frank and his family wanted to skirt the law, there was absolutely no room to run on this bridge without seriously risking their lives.

Frank's dad sprang into action. Sonny crossed the road approaching the bridge to use a pay phone. The glass surrounding the booth was cracked, garbage strewn about the floor, the door hanging on its hinges. He dialed the local police and waited for a call back from the captain. The phone rang. Sonny sweet-talked the captain into allowing the crew to pass over, and before he could even reach the motor home across the road, Elizabeth police arrived on the scene. They gave the go-ahead to bridge personnel and provided Frank an escort over the Goethals and into Staten Island, New York, the twelfth and final state. New York City police picked up the escort near the Verrazano-Narrows. Approaching the bridge, John steered his bike in front of the black and white police car with its overhead lights flashing.

"God," Frank beamed, "we are coming home."

The uncertainty of Frank's arrival time made it difficult for even family and friends to share in the moment. A few folks arrived from United Way. But Frank's friends and family made plans to attend the ceremonial finish the following day.

"I was too exhausted to care," Frank said.

He cared. Frank felt somewhat hollow on that early evening when he crossed the official finish line on the Verrazano-Narrows Bridge, setting a world record for running across the United States of America. The time: 46 days, 8 hours, 36 minutes, 25 seconds. The distance: 3,103 miles. The miles-per-day average used as Guinnesss' measuring stick: 66.94 miles.

Frank had run 73.6 miles his final day.

Cottrell's record of 64.56 miles per day was gone. It was time for Frank to rejoice in a hard-to-describe feeling of triumph, his goal conquered, his life regaining direction and equilibrium after years of bouncing around like Bingo balls.

Only he couldn't muster the feeling he deserved to hold.

The world-record holder felt empty.

Why? How?

Frank's finish was devoid of a crucial element. He had his immediate family by his side. But he was without the bond of female companionship integral to his existence. There was no Hollywood ending with the girlfriend waiting at the finish line to jump into the arms of her hero.

There was no Patty Whelan, the one who got away and had inadvertently spurred Frank, needing the distraction and clarity of running more than ever, to run across the country for the first time more than a year earlier. Frank felt more alone than ever. Maybe it was the residue of doldrums often associated with ultra-marathon runs, or the fact that a formal ceremony would take place the following day.

Or not. Maybe the run wouldn't impact Frank the way he had envisioned. There was nothing mandating that lives change, no less improve, from running long distances, even across the country, even in world-record time. Maybe the whole thing represented one wacky adventure.

And little else.

"It was anticlimactic, to be honest," Frank said of crossing the finish line. "I was euphoric. But I don't remember being confident or fulfilled. I just remember that the job was over."

It was an oddly nondescript finish. Festivities the following day left Frank another night, and a 9.9-mile run to the Brooklyn Bridge, to discover context. Little did Frank know that he would spend the rest of his life searching for perspective and purpose, that such feelings can prove elusive despite spending forty-six days and 3,103 miles sorting through issues.

AAU and United Way, meantime, had engaged in their own battle for sponsorship space on Frank's body for the ceremonial finish. The groups sparred over which logo would adorn Frank's official finish-line shirt and hat. Both organizations wanted top billing on the shirt. There even had been talk of giving both sponsors equal play on the shirt, a cluttered look that Frank detested.

AAU Shoes ultimately won out on the T-shirt, which explained the very '70s white tee with AAU SHOES in blue across the front, the AAU USA logo underneath and a half-inch red-trimmed neckline and half-inch red-trimmed sleeve endings. United Way got the hat. And the finish-line banner read "AAU Shoes Run Coast to Coast."

About fifty members of the media and twenty to thirty family and friends joined United Way officials the following day to await Frank's ceremonial finish on the Brooklyn Bridge. He stopped on the bridge to take the bottle of water John had filled from the Pacific Ocean less than two months earlier in San Francisco. Frank tossed it toward the East River, but another casualty of the run, a right arm devoid of strength, left him short on the throw. The bottle shattered on the lower deck of the bridge and droplets fell into the river.

Yet another problem. Frank was fifteen minutes early for his scheduled arrival and the media had yet to fully assemble. A United Way official had Frank, John and Bogdan hide behind bridge girders to await the media. The media arrived and the trio approached the finish line. They were about to cross the tape when somebody yelled "CUT!" The press photographers apparently weren't satisfied with the finish-line shot.

"I think they dropped the finish-line banner prematurely," Frank said.

Frank, John and Bogdan backtracked to re-do the finish. They were a few steps from crossing the line, the final finish line, when they heard another scream from the crowd.

"HOLD IT!"

It was Shapiro, the film producer. He had noticed Bogdan wearing New Balance shoes, not exactly an AAU advertising strategy the company had sought. Bogdan slithered off to the side of the finish-line banner.

Finally, on the third take, Frank Giannino officially/unofficially finished his record-breaking run across the United States.

There was perhaps no moment in his entire existence that more acutely captured Frank's imperfections. Even in setting a world record, even through no fault of his own, Frank couldn't get the finish right.

He again felt empty despite family members and friends making the ninety-minute drive down from the Hudson Valley. There was a brief ceremony. The Gianninos walked to City Hall a half-mile away for a press conference on the steps of the mayoral building. City officials heaped praise on Frank's amazing run, though precisely like his starting-line ceremony, the mayor, in this case Ed Koch, was absent, said to be out of town on business.

"I look forward to the day when I can share these experiences with all of you," Frank said.

The press conference ended and Frank's old buddy from New Paltz, Bob Bright, handed Frank a bottle of Molson Golden Ale outside the motor home. Frank drank the beer, stepped into the vehicle and fell into a deep sleep. He was sleeping as the motor home navigated its way out of New York City and headed northwest toward Orange County.

Running can provide an intense feeling of euphoria. The runner's high is real and powerful, and just imagine the inner buzz after breaking a three thousand-mile world record.

But there is another overwhelming feeling that ultra and adventure runners typically keep to themselves. It occurs when an especially grueling race is over, even with goals fulfilled, and runners smack into a mean case of the blues. Sometimes the doldrums creep in shortly past the finish line, sometimes the next day, sometimes weeks or decades later. Sometimes the feeling is every bit as low as the high of reaching the finish, like coming down from the most powerful stimulant, from feeling atop the world to sinking into a tunnel of emptiness.

Frank's depressive state had gotten an early start. He felt down the moment he crossed the finish line the previous day.

"It was jubilation," he said, "but a death."

A death? Frank's second run was supposed to be about unscrambling his life. He had just set a world record. He had his whole life in front of him. How could he be feeling so bleak?

"Because," Frank said, "I knew I would never do it again. I knew for the rest of my life, I would never top it."

What Frank didn't know was just how much pain he would endure chasing finish lines for the rest of his life.

Frank and his crew on the steps of City Hall, New York City, after his ceremonial finish. From left, his dad Sonny, Frank, step-mom Ja, and brother John.

17

Now What?

Frank Giannino had twice accomplished his dream of running across the United States. He had reached his ultimate goal of setting the world record. Now he had to figure out what to do with his life. This course would be as difficult as any three thousand-miler, but more treacherous.

"I had no plan," Frank said. "While on the roads, I just thought about the daily grind."

Ultra runners before and after Frank parlayed their adventures into fame, in some cases even fortune. They wrote books. They became sought-after public speakers. They operated successful businesses. They learned to use the Internet freeway for purposes of marketing and self-promotion and business entities.

They made money.

Dean Karnazes became the poster boy for using his business acumen and running skills to make a buck. He set up his own business. He worked for Fortune 500 companies. He even made *Time* magazine's "Top 100 Most Influential People in the World" list in 2006.

Karnazes' first book, *Ultra Marathon Man: Confessions of an All-Night Runner*, became a *New York Times* best seller. His motivational speeches commanded up to $25,000.

Frank never expected to have the kind of post-running success of Karnazes or others. For one, Frank didn't have their running chops. Karnazes brought a long list of running accomplishments. Frank was a low-30s 10K runner and a top-notch marathoner, but his running fame started and ended with two runs across the country. He was as faceless as many others on the pages of the *Guinness Book*, not quite as anonymous as the world record-holder for largest tongue, or the woman with the longest fingernails, but largely unknown nonetheless.

Frank wanted to bask in the glory of his achievements. He wanted to earn a living off of running. But he had virtually no idea how to go about it.

So Frank's post-run speaking engagements – all gratis – featured stops at kids' groups and fund raisers and Rotary gatherings and Lions Club meetings. He was a big man on campus, but the campus was a relatively minuscule swath of land in Hudson Valley, New York. There were no Fortune 500 companies ringing Frank's phone, no major publishers beating down his door for his story.

Frank running to Dietz Stadium in Kingston, New York, for a Frank Giannino Day celebrating his record-breaking run.

The summer following his first run, in 1979, Frank worked on a book with a local author named Franklin Stevens. Stevens had produced sixty pages and an outline for the rest when Frank started having difficulty reaching the author. The project eventually ended when Frank lost contact with Stevens.

In the fall of 1980 following the second crossing, Sandra Zerbe, representing a local printing company called Pyr Press, rifled through Frank's record-setting run to produce a manuscript in weeks. The book would be called *The Rogue Runner*. A brochure was published and, according to Frank, a half-dozen copies or so were pre-sold.

But the book was never published. According to Pyr owner Carol Boyle, the book was supposed to be underwritten by Frank's sponsor, Intermark, and the company would purchase twenty-five thousand copies to help promote Frank and the AAU Shoes brand. Boyle said she got no response after the book was sent to Frank's sponsors, and then received a cool reception from Intermark upon visiting its corporate headquarters in Cleveland. Intermark was dissatisfied with the content of the book, Boyle said, and she was told no thanks when she offered a re-write.

The Rogue Runner, in Boyle's words, was dead.

Somewhere lost in the process were two shoe boxes filled with photos of the run. Boyle said neither she nor her husband remember seeing the boxes. Frank thinks they became a victim of the Pyr building burning down.

Frank had a gift for gab and salesmanship. But he lacked technical skills and the confidence to master them in a world rapidly becoming dependent on them for promotion of any kind. He knew little about marketing and promotion. He had a phobia – his word – for computers, eliminating a vital tool for successful business models.

Still, Frank's greatest liability in adulthood was the same problem he faced from his earliest childhood. He lacked the confidence and self-esteem to chase his dream with the same vigor that he had chased the world record for fastest run across America. He was still, in many ways, the conservative hippie content to travel the country, bedding down in his red VW van adorned with blue curtains and white trim on the hood and around the windows.

Only now he was pushing thirty years old.

Frank's first crack at turning his record-breaking run into a career came shortly after his finish. He met with representatives from Intermark in Cleveland to discuss designing shoes for the company. But Frank's lack of inner belief reared its head once again.

"I had brought a bunch of samples from different shoe companies," Frank said. "They had a factory rep from Korea there. I talked about my experience and what I thought the shoe should be. They made me a trainer shoe and racing flat. But the shoes never got manufactured."

Frank designed two pairs of low-impact shoes for a show in Las Vegas the following January. He didn't think Intermark had a team in place to build a new shoe line. After he left Las Vegas, Frank said he never heard from the company again. It didn't matter. He didn't feel comfortable or qualified doing the job anyway.

He talked about partnering with buddy Bob Bright, who had become sole owner of the running store in New Paltz called Catch Us If You Can Running Center. Frank thought he was receiving a $10,000 lump-sum payment from his sponsor, Intermark, but instead got $750 monthly installments for a year. He didn't have the funding to join Bright.

Frank met with John Szefc, then publisher of the *Times Herald-Record*, a mid-sized newspaper in Middletown. Szefc had contacted Frank a month before his cross-country run asking if he would like to help start a road race in the city to celebrate the newspaper's twenty-fifth anniversary. Frank brought Bright to the organizational meeting, and Bright suggested having a 10K and inviting Frank Shorter, who grew up in Middletown. The committee also invited Shorter rival Bill Rodgers, who dueled with Shorter for most of the inaugural Orange Classic 10K in 1981 before succumbing to the hometown hero in the final half mile. Shorter and Rodgers helped build the race into one of the top road races in the Northeast for years to come, as listed by *Runner's World* magazine.

The paper paid Frank $2,500 to help form and direct the first race. But the closest Frank got to a formal position at the paper was to become its freelance running columnist five months after his record-breaking crossing. Again, Frank was unqualified to run a marketing department and unable to muster the confidence to learn on the run.

Frank was invited to be a full-time host of the nightly telecast for a new station in Middletown called Cable 6. It was owned by Alan Gerry, a local billionaire who had pioneered cable TV in the 1950s. Once more, the opportunity failed to grow into anything substantial.

"What I knew was that, through my accomplishments, I had bought freedom," Frank said. "I earned the freedom to do what I wanted to do every day of my life because of those two runs."

What he hadn't earned was the knowledge to make a living through the runs. In the summer of '81, on the afternoon of the Orange Classic road race, Frank met up with an avid runner named Bruce Birnbaum.

"What are you doing for the rest of your life?" Birnbaum asked Frank Giannino.

Talk about a loaded question. Frank was unsure what he was doing for the rest of the afternoon. Birnbaum had co-founded the local running club, Orange Runners, in 1980. He wanted to partner with Frank in a running shoe store in Middletown called "Blisters Ltd,'' a thousand-square-foot bottom-floor space with no store front.

"This was a sincere, honest guy who you knew if you did something with him, he'd never hurt you," Birnbaum said of Frank, "and he didn't."

Birnbaum bankrolled the operation and the business was up and running within a month of Birnbaum posing that question to Frank. Within a year, Birnbaum's marriage ended in divorce and the business fizzled.

"The store closing had nothing to do with Frank," Birnbaum said. "I have never enjoyed losing so much money in all my life than in working with Frank. It was just a grand time. He taught me everything about shoes. He could look at old shoes and tell you exactly what's wrong with you. He just knows feet. He doesn't need a podiatry degree or anything. He is as knowledgeable as anyone, in my opinion.

"It was kind of therapy for me, if you will," Birnbaum said. "He took my mind off other things."

Frank became a full-time substitute teacher for a year at his alma mater school district just outside Middletown. But he did it mostly for a paycheck. His heart wasn't into teaching. His heart was into running. He just couldn't figure out how to live off the sport.

Frank returned to his roots. He wasn't going to get rich putting on local races, but fulfillment comes in many forms. Frank became adept at laying out routes and certifying courses. He organized the Old Mine Road 100K from Kingston – New York's first capital – to Port Jervis, an old railroad town twenty miles from Middletown. It was hardly groundbreaking stuff, but he loved it.

In 1983, a local businessman named Al Weinert, sponsor of the 100K, became handshake partners with Frank on another running store, this one in downtown Middletown. Weinert bankrolled the store, called "Frank's Run-In Room."

Frank was back in business. But he had already learned that the life of a small businessman was filled with those familiar feelings of uncertainty, anxiety and fear.

Those same emotions would engulf both his professional *and* personal life across the next decade.

The world record-breaking runner was soon on the verge of going broke.

18

A Miracle

What had become of Frank Giannino? Where were the riches that he had hoped would follow the run of a lifetime?

Who was this guy?

Fifteen years.

Fifteen years since breaking the world record for fastest run across the United States. Fifteen years and Frank had two defining failures:

Bad business decisions leaving him in financial distress.

And finally, a failed marriage.

Frank's other woman in the marriage was his business. He worked seven days a week and brought home the stress of trying to pay the bills. He would meet his wife at work and close shop, but open back up if a customer pulled into the parking lot as they headed out, then keep her waiting while he closed the sale.

Anything for the sale.

Frank viewed his work ethic as essential to making money and keeping customers satisfied. He grew up seeing conflict between his own parents over money problems. Frank wanted to do everything he could to avoid those same issues driving a wedge through his family. Instead, Frank's long hours became a burden on his family and the money woes hit rock bottom. There were times in the Giannino household when they had to scrounge up enough money for food. Money had become the dominant issue in Frank's marriage, just as it was with his parents growing up. Asked how his day went upon arriving at home each night, Frank gave a sales figure. That's how his day went. The pressure of maintaining a profitable business was intense.

Frank skimmed from the business for six months to help keep up with family expenses. He said he wound up taking five years to repay Weinert the five-figure sum. But Frank's efforts to make amends left him stressed and distant. He bordered on depressed. The business remained on shaky footing.

Frank said he had Weinert paid in full by the 1990s, and that Weinert signed off the business to Frank in 1993. Frank took over the store.

In 1995, he was on the cusp of going out of business. His inventory was down to ten cases of shoes. And then, out of the blue, a customer walked in showing off a neat orthotic that Frank had never seen. The man was from California. He told Frank about the product, called Superfeet.

Frank was fascinated. He had to try out these Superfeet himself. So Frank had the man watch the store while he inserted the orthotic and went for a four-mile run.

"I immediately felt like I was home," Frank said.

Frank called the company that made the product, only to learn that its representatives included none other than Chris Smith. He was the professor at California College of Podiatric Medicine who, along with colleague Richard Bogdan, had evaluated Frank days before his second run and concluded, "You are not going to finish this thing."

This time, however, Frank didn't ignore Smith's suggestion. Frank ordered his first shipment of Superfeet. Customers fell in love with the product and Frank had a second wind. All Superfeet did was save Frank's store, maybe save Frank from bankruptcy and years of hardship, while providing a long-term marketing model for subsequent businesses.

But just about the time Frank found the jewel that would brighten things financially, his deteriorating marriage had reached the point of no return.

Frank's ten-year union, long in a state of erosion, was about to officially end.

Frank was more confused and disappointed than shocked and angry by the failed marriage. He felt relieved that he would no longer have to survive the emotional turbulence the union had wrought. He was, in a sense, back on the roads navigating miles. One foot after another. One mile at a time.

"I went into survival mode again," he said of the divorce. "I just look at the challenges facing me, whether it's a running challenge or a family challenge."

The relationship wasn't all bad. There were two little angels from the marriage. One was Caitlin Giannino, arriving on May 26, 1987. The other was the couple's miracle baby, Hope Giannino, checking in on Oct. 10, 1990.

Hope's name became as much a symbol of her own uncertain arrival as it was of Frank's perpetually promising outlook throughout his problematic life. She wasn't supposed to make it. A sonogram showed signs of her never reaching birth. The next sonogram showed things to be normal. And finally, she survived a risky delivery and was born perfectly healthy.

Caitlin has pointed to the period following her parents' divorce – 1997-99 – as some of the best and most memorable days she had with her dad. Four years younger, Hope has a fuzzier recollection. But Frank and the girls spent many weekends together on various camping trips in New York's Adirondack Mountains or cruising to Martha's Vineyard in Massachusetts or going whale watching in nearby Cape Cod. He was able to share road trips with his children that he had been unable to experience in his own childhood. Their bond tightened.

Caitlin and Hope went on to have a solid relationship with both their parents. The girls lived with their mother a few minutes away for much of their school years. Caitlin graduated magna cum laude from East Stroudsburg (Pennsylvania) University. She pursued a career in teaching and, in July 2012, was married. Hope graduated from SUNY Orange, the junior college in Middletown, and transferred to SUNY New Paltz, both schools among her dad's college stops. Caitlin and Hope matured into beautiful and healthy young women.

"They are ten times the people I'll ever be," Frank said.

When he wasn't spending time with his children, Frank was

focusing on work and his involvement in the local running community. He was having his teeth cleaned one day when the dentist shared details of the woman he believed to be a perfect match for Frank. Only days later, the woman, a middle-aged single mother of two named Michele Blampied, posed a question to the dentist a question while getting her own teeth cleaned.

"You are a young professional," she said to Dr. Frank Giorgianni. "Don't you have any friends?"

In fact, Dr. Giorgianni and wife Mary had discussed matching Michele and Frank. When he finished cleaning Michele's teeth, Dr. Giorgianni led her to his office and called Frank. Michele and Frank set up a date.

It was the summer of '99 and Michele couldn't wait to share the news. She stepped from the office and pulled out her cell phone in the parking lot to call one of Frank's customers and biggest fans, Walter Blampied – her dad.

"Because," Michele explained, "my dad loved Frank."

Michele was born in Middletown and had something of a nomadic upbringing as the family often relocated to satisfy her dad's job as a plumber. "We were like Chevy Chase," Michele said. "My parents would throw us in the car. One job transfer was to Galveston, Texas. We were there for three-quarters of the school year, January to May (during Michele's freshman year). We were the only white kids on the bus and always picked last for teams in gym class."

From there, the family traveled to the Grand Canyon. "It was like a big family adventure. We were on the road for three months. We lived in Illinois in July and August; my dad had a job in Peoria."

She was the second oldest of four children, two boys and two girls. Her parents ended up divorcing after twenty-five years of marriage. Her dad remarried and not long ago celebrated a second twenty-fifth anniversary. Her mom didn't remarry and has enjoyed retirement.

All four of the Blampied children have been divorced.

"I guess we are all wonderfully dysfunctional," Michele laughed.

A teacher, Michele had more in common with Frank than having their teeth cleaned by the same dentist. Long before they met, she often gave her dad, a running enthusiast who ran the New York City Marathon at age 57, gift cards for Frank's store. She would hand her dad a card and tell him, "Go see your buddy."

They had met before Dr. Giorgianni played matchmaker. In the spring of 1981, Frank had just finished his record-breaking run and Michele, nine years younger, was finishing up college. She had just completed a five-mile run with a brother-in-law at the time, and they topped it off with a drink at a local bar. At the bar they ran into Frank, whom her brother-in-law knew. He introduced Frank to Michele.

"Oh, are you a runner?" Michele asked. "What's the farthest distance you have run?"

Told that he had run across the country twice and held the record for fastest crossing, Michele's face turned red. But she dismissed any potential for a love connection. This guy, Michele had decided, was out of her league.

More than a decade later, Michele's marriage started to disintegrate around the same time as Frank's. She was separated in 1997.

Michele didn't see anyone for a year and a half after breaking up with her ex. She had too much to protect, namely her two young children and a lovely home in Johnson, New York, just outside Middletown. Michele was so protective that when a friend finally talked her into going on a blind date, she laid down firm ground rules. There would be no discussing her children or where she lived. She went on a few dates and spent eight largely disinterested months with the guy.

"He's as exciting to you as white mayonnaise on white bread," a friend told Michele. "What you're looking for is the Italian sub."

"Does that mean I'm going to start dating Italians?" Michele laughed.

Dr. Giorgianni set up things a bit later. Michele and Frank decided on a night out at a bar/restaurant in New Paltz.

"It was nice," Michele said. "I found myself talking about my kids. He took out this picture and showed me. 'These are my babies; these are my daughters. I love my kids.' My dating rules went out the window. Everything that I felt strongly about was gone before the end of the first date. We were able to really dedicate our time together those first few weeks."

Even Michele's ex had a soft spot for Frank. When the guy delayed in signing divorce papers, Michele said, Frank offered to help expedite the process. "Let me do it," Frank told Michele.

According to Michele, Frank met with her ex to get him to sign the papers. "You gotta' do what's right," Frank told the man. Frank used his charm and diplomacy, according to Michele, but her ex said there was not a notary public available to witness the signing. So Frank drove to the police station to get a notary. Told the notary would be unavailable for an hour, Frank took the ex out to eat. They returned to the police station, and within minutes Michele Blampied officially had her divorce.

"We were on the same page," Frank said. "The issues in our lives seemed minuscule because she was so easy to be with and to talk to. She has a gift for a clear view of things. She can see what's going on and can communicate it in a way that is absolutely right on. I can see why she is such a great teacher."

In the first week of August 2000, a year after they met, Michele and Frank traveled to Mount Rainier in Washington. They joined a mountaineering course in hiking to Camp Muir, and before dropping out of the course at six thousand feet elevation, Frank got on one knee in front of Michele as the group looked on.

"I chose Rainier because it was the most beautiful place I have ever been to in my life," Frank said. "I wanted to make a memory that she would never forget."

Michele said yes, a commitment that restored a measure of luck to Frank's life. On July 7, 2001, two years to the day after they had met, Michele Blampied and Frank Giannino III were married.

Michele had found her Italian sub.

"She is the perfect fit," Frank said. "She is beautiful; I love to look at her. We can talk about anything. We laugh every day

135

about something. We hardly ever argue. Our only disagreements in the past were about our ex-spouses. Trust, loyalty and honesty remain way up there on our list of expectations. We are dedicated to the marriage and to one another. We are dedicated to our children."

Marijean, once bitter toward her brother, had become both a mother figure to Frank after Ruth's passing and, much like Sonny, a confidante to Frank. So it was fitting that Marijean walked Frank down the aisle.

The reception was in the backyard of Michele's home, now their home, as friends and family stripped down to their casuals. Only one person had a problem with the day. Michele's daughter Samantha knew her mom and Frank were leaving on their honeymoon, a cruise to Bermuda, the next day. Only ten, Samantha showed that even the healthiest kids fret over the arrival of step dads. In her case, Samantha worried that Frank wasn't going to bring back her mommy.

"I love you," Michele told Samantha over and over. "I will always come back."

Michele and Frank felt like a couple of kids in love. They joined Michele's father and step mom on the cruise, in addition to two other couples and friends of the family. When it came time to meet for meals, the big question around the table was whether Michele and Frank were going to show up. They maximized their alone time.

The newlyweds returned home and took a few days before heading back out, this time with their four kids on a family honeymoon. They flew to Las Vegas, where Michele and Frank rented a motor home. In déjà vu fashion, the ride overheated and rat-a-tat-tatted much of their two-week three thousand-mile jaunt visiting the national parks.

"He's a father, but he's also a stepfather of two kids who think the world of him," Michele said. "They've always liked Frank. It's hard not to like Frank."

Michele counted only one knock-down, drag-out fight with Frank in all their years together. "The thing with Frank is, he doesn't fight people," she said. "Frank just wants to make people happy. I think at times he's been taken advantage of. He doesn't like conflict. I'd have to seriously push his buttons to get him upset."

And when Frank did get upset, when his life seemed unfulfilled and darkness came over him, Michele was there to hold him up. She was the new leader of his support team, Frank's new savior. And like those final days running across America when brother John and Sonny saved Frank from quitting, Michele would breathe life into Frank when he hit rock bottom.

19

Quitting Worse than Dying

Frank (Sonny) Giannino Jr. was determined to prevent the family from incurring massive health care costs as he became sick. He had witnessed too much unnecessary spending as a male nurse, and two and a half decades earlier, bills from Ruth's sickness totaled some $190,000. Only $100,000 of it was covered by insurance, leaving Sonny to take out a new mortgage on their paid-off home in Walden to cover the costs.

He had moved to Florida in the late 1980s and had heart surgery in 1990. Sonny was going to make sure that neither man nor machine prolonged his life.

Frank's dad seemed fine during much of 2000. That is why Frank didn't hesitate to take his extended family to Disney World for Easter vacation that year. Michele and her biological children, Samantha and Glenn, went on the trip, as well as Frank's daughter Hope. Caitlin, his oldest daughter, stayed behind after being released from the hospital. She'd had meningitis. Brother John, the Iron Man, and his family went on the trip as well. They visited Sonny, the record-breaking crew chief, on their way home from Disney World. He seemed okay.

Frank was at his store one October day in 2000 when he received a call from Ja. His dad was about to go on dialysis. Doctors were giving him six weeks to live.

It was an oddly familiar scenario to Frank who, twenty-six years earlier while stationed in the Army, had gotten the telegram from Dad announcing his mom's grave condition. This time the call came from Ja, though she shared the news much more quickly than her husband had with Ruth. "There had been no symptoms or signs of problems," Frank said.

Sonny spent the final six weeks of his life with maybe one or two hours of consciousness. Frank stayed with his dad for eight days before returning home to Orange County. Frank's four siblings, living in parts of California and New York, also visited their dad in his final days.

During that last trip to visit Dad, Sonny had a message for his oldest son and Frank drew close to listen.

"Thank God," Sonny said, referencing the greatest joint venture of their lives, "we did that, Frank."

Sonny insisted on spending his last days at home. Frank's oldest sister Marijean, her relationship with Dad often fractured, was at his home when he went into the bathroom and pulled out his stent. Typical Sonny. He planned to go out on his terms. Marijean and Nancy had been about to leave his room when he made a request.

"I'd love to have a beer," he said.

Nancy went and got her father a beer. He drank a few sips and went to the bathroom, then returned to bed. A little while later, on Dec. 2, 2000, Nancy held him in her arms when Sonny took his final breath. He was seventy-eight.

"He was in control until the end," Marijean told Frank. "Unbelievable!"

Support is needed to navigate the various obstacles of daily life, not just while running across the country. Frank desperately needed support to reach the treasure chest of finish lines when the crowds stopped cheering. The decade following Sonny's death tested Frank's inner strength as firmly as either run across the country. Soon after his dad passed away, Frank got a phone call from Marijean. She had drawn a startling conclusion from therapy.

"I found out what my problem was," she told Frank.

"What's that?" he responded.

"You."

Marijean had resented Frank in his early years, tying him to her strained relationship with Dad. It was as if she knew from

Day One that Frank would become another obstacle in her love-hate relationship with Sonny.

"He's a really ugly baby," sister Barbara remembers Marijean saying the first time she saw her newest sibling in the hospital.

Marijean's bitterness toward Frank intensified as his relationship with Dad blossomed. She felt her father was a control freak, a side that Frank had never recognized or chosen to recognize. Marijean's thoughts and feelings toward her father grew complicated over the years. Was she being too hard on him? Overreacting to his faults? One thing she believed without a doubt: Her dad's marriage to Ja six months after Ruth's death came way too soon, despite her admiration for Ja and Ja's healthy relationship with the Giannino siblings.

Frank was hurt by Marijean's declaration. Ever the pleaser, he had spent his earliest days trying to impress his oldest sister and her friends. Of course, Marijean came in especially handy when inviting female friends over for pajama parties as Frank, forever girl crazy, approached the titillating times of adolescence. Her friends enjoyed the added entertainment and innocently poked fun at Frank, who drew revenge by chasing them around the house carrying garter snakes. Some of Marijean's friends still remember calling Frank Snake Boy.

Marijean became something of a hippie. In 1969, she attended the second day of the Woodstock Festival, only a couple exits off the New York State Thruway from the Gianninos. Marijean and Frank were on opposite ends of the political spectrum, she more a liberal, he more a conservative with some liberal tendencies. But their relationship, despite Marijean's inner turmoil, had grown into a tight bond over the years. Marijean was the one, after all, who wired Frank $300 after her broke teen brother called following an impulsive hitchhike to Florida over spring break '71 with buddy John Santacroce.

Marijean was the one who, along with Barbara, was ready to take Frank AWOL to Canada in '72 after he received orders to go to Vietnam. The plan thankfully was squashed the same day when Frank's orders were canceled by President Nixon when he froze the deployment of troops.

Marijean, six years older, was the one who became a mother figure to Frank after Ruth died. He often called her just to talk, unlike so many siblings who allow time and distance to win the day. He felt comfortable discussing anything with Marijean.

It was why Frank felt incredibly deep pain the day he learned Marijean had been diagnosed with the same disease that killed their mom. Breast cancer.

Marijean had a radical mastectomy followed by chemotherapy. Years went by and she was diagnosed with cancer again. This time they found lesions on her brain. She spent time in and out of the hospital until, on Oct. 23, 2006, Marijean Giannino passed away at age 60.

"There isn't a day that goes by that I don't miss her," Frank said. "She was a great big sister."

***

Marijean's death came during Frank's peak years in business. He had sought to change his work-obsessed ways after meeting Michele. She loved Frank for his tenderness and caring, his zest for life and adventure and travel. They went on vacations early in the marriage, taking the kids to Hershey Park in Pennsylvania, to Disney a couple of times. They went on a European vacation, flying into France and England and Scotland, spending their last four days at the Royal Edinburgh Military Tattoo, a summer-long festival. They renewed their vows at the Gretna Green, the Las Vegas of the UK just over the border in Scotland.

"In the first five, six years of being with Frank," Michele said, "he was always passionate about travel; 'I want to do this and that.'"

That all started to change in late 2004. Seeking to expand his store, Frank closed on a larger building, a former 7-Eleven virtually across the street from his business in the Town of Wallkill, which neighbors Middletown.

"When we bought the store, I felt this is what he deserves," Michele said. "This is the epitome of this man's business. He had been doing this for years; he had been renting from Weinert. I felt this was the next level for him in his career, in his life, and in his business.

"And he's so good at it. He loves to talk. He is his happiest when that store is packed and he's the center of attention and he's educating people and light-heartedly poking fun at people. Telling a wife her husband has girly feet. He's so scripted. He knows what to say. He's so passionate. That's why there's so much to love about him."

As he did in his first marriage, Frank's focus turned almost exclusively to work after moving into the larger building. The vacations stopped. The alone time with Michele all but ended.

"The piece that I'm missing is my time with him," Michele said. "The Michele and Frank time has become non-existent. I'll say, 'How was your day?' and he'll give me a number of cash sales. He's got a lot of people tugging at him. A lot. And all he does is work seven days a week. But he gets up every day. He's positive. He's optimistic. He knows what he has to do. He's focused. He's friendly. I don't know how he does it."

Michele provided a healthy balance for Frank. While Frank avoided confrontation at almost all cost, Michele could be feisty. In fact, her assertiveness probably ultimately helped save his livelihood. The new business added immeasurable stress to Frank's life. Frank took on the building expenses alone despite consultants telling him to assume a partner or lease a portion of the large structure. The overhead was astronomical, enlivening his insecurities and fears.

"I was in love with the dream of owning my own building," he said. "It was like a marriage."

Frank closed on the building on Dec. 7, 2004. That night, he put his head on his pillow and felt a dizzying onslaught of stress and anxiety. Frank barely slept that night and many more nights for the next six years. He relied on sleeping pills for about a year while Michele worried he'd become addicted to them. He even complained of chest pains a couple times.

"I had this overwhelming feeling of stress," he said. "I always had insecurity, and I think it all stemmed from a lack of organizational skills. For the first time in my life, I was out of control. I was in over my head. When I ran across the country, though scared to death, I was never in over my head."

Things started well enough after Frank opened the new store,

Frank's Custom Shoe-Fitting, in July 2005. The business grew every year from 2006 to 2008. But the overhead and a sagging economy inevitably put Frank in serious debt.

"The whole time, I was like the skipper of the Titanic," Frank said. "I felt something wrong, but I felt helpless to stop it."

Frank's cash-flow problems started to cost him valuable inventory. Customers were Frank's lifeline, but many disappeared as inventory dwindled. People came in looking for products that Frank didn't have in stock. He promised to order their product but often encountered problems in shipment because of money owed to companies. New Balance, for example, wanted the $10,000 owed to the company or promised to close his account. Customers disappeared after growing weary of waiting weeks for a pair of sneakers. Frank figured that he lost five hundred customers in two years. He feared that he would never get them back again. Frank borrowed $16,500 from friends to help pay some of his debt, mostly, he said, "to keep the business above water."

"I didn't have any shoes," Frank said. "My inventory was depleted my last three years there."

Frank needed a bank loan. But it was the absolute worst time to secure a loan with the economy in shambles largely due to banking failures. Five banks in two weeks turned down his bid to refinance. One bank said yes and strung him along for six months. Inventory continued to dwindle, testing the loyalty of customer relations he had developed over more than two decades.

"I was in that position because of my stubbornness," he said. "I could have gotten out (of the building) long ago. But that stubbornness is also what allowed me to do those runs."

He tortured himself for not buying an affordable building that had become available five years earlier in a nearby town. On Oct. 27, 2004, the same night the Red Sox beat the Cardinals in Game Four to win the World Series for the first time in eighty-six years, Michele and Frank had decided to purchase a store called Sneakers to Boots in a town not far from Frank's current business. Frank could have had the building if he'd paid some cash up front to secure a contract. But another couple showed up with the money and that was it. Another questionable business decision in Frank's flawed folder.

"It would have been different," he said about owning that business twenty-five minutes from Middletown. "But my community involvement would have been different. I may not have gotten involved with the (Orange) Classic," the local road race he had helped spawn.

In August 2009, Frank formally decided to try selling the building. He had the worst fall of his life, a thirty percent drop in business from the previous year. Bankruptcy was not an option because, like his two greatest running accomplishments, "I had faith in myself to finish.

"People go through bankruptcy because they quit," he said, slapping his hand on the table to make the point. "I've always looked at everything as goals and projects, even in my business life. You are going to survive it and make it, or give it up.

"Quitting is worse than dying to me."

Two months later, Michele and Frank met with two bank employees to discuss his debts. The bankers pushed three letters in front of Michele and Frank, according to the couple. One included details of their foreclosing on their home. The other two envelopes involved signing off on the two loans Frank had on the building. Frank broke down and cried. He couldn't remember ever being so emotional. Frank saw his entire life flowing into an ocean of failure and self-pity.

"He was crumbling," Michele said. "I had never seen anybody able to break down Frank like that."

Frank quickly was reminded that every journey needs a support team. This time, it was a team of one: Michele.

"There is no way you are taking my house!" she told the bank employee. Michele picked Frank off the ground, almost literally, wrung him out and continued hammering the bankers.

The bank gave Frank six months to come up with the money.

"I question my worth," Frank said at the time. "I resent it because I shouldn't be in this position at this stage of my life. Three of my buddies are retired. I lose four to six sales a day because of a lack of inventory. It's been the longest cross-America run ever – the hardest one yet. It's my life path that set this all up. I came in without a plan."

Frank was about as down as he could get. He tried to keep smiling, tried to ignore the pain, when he realized he had run up against a familiar feeling. Frank decided that he would no longer helplessly watch his business fail. He redirected the challenge to a familiar goal.

Frank visualized being in the middle of his third run across the United States. "I'm in Iowa," he would say cheerfully inside his store. "I'm in Ohio," he would report on another day. Slowly but with renewed vigor, he was getting himself to the finish line. And like his actual three thousand-mile runs, Frank was going to fight like hell to the end.

"I have a very clear view about who I am, where I am at, at this point of my life," he said with the building up for sale. "I've never doubted what I'm all about. I just got sucked into the dream and nobody tried to stop it – none of us tried to stop it. The worst-case scenario is that I'm going to take a huge hit (on the sale). But I believe I'm going to come out with my business, my character and my reputation intact, even if I have to leave the location and move into another location nearby.

"I just want to concentrate on selling product," Frank said. "The business has always been there, but I'm too distracted by too many factors. I'm seeing twenty percent every month going to rent. You can't run a business like that.

"When I did my two runs, I found out how to do it and succeeded and got all the right collaborators beyond my family, and figured out all the external factors. My big albatross has not been the task at hand; it's been the bank holding this tremendous burden over me and all the choices I made along with that. That's the source of all our stress.

"I have to change at age fifty-seven. I'm in Illinois now; I'm in Chicago Heights. I was doing my best running when (Stan) Cottrell showed up."

Frank endured a few false hopes on prospective sales before a buyer finally emerged in early 2010. The sales price was $400,000, $50,000 less than what Frank had asked. But it allowed Frank to escape much of his debt and move to a smaller building a quarter-mile away on the same side of the same road.

Frank had failed at trying to prosper with a large store. He would have to make it with a small store and modest overhead. Frank decided that sometimes, unlike running three thousand miles, smaller is indeed better.

He kept the name, Frank's Custom Shoe-Fitting, and focused on perfecting his preferred business plan of selling running shoes and creating custom orthotics. A certified pedorthist, Frank got involved in a potentially lucrative program that gives diabetics shoes once a year with Medicare footing the bill.

Frank was about to turn fifty-nine and, once again, he was reinventing himself. He was excited about the new adventure. He had a viable business again.

Frank seemed on the cusp of losing something else, however; perhaps something more meaningful, if not more valuable, than his livelihood.

His world record for the fastest run across the United States was being challenged.

20

Record in Jeopardy

Some 252 people have run across the country 283 times starting with the first recorded run by Edward Payson Weston in 1909, according to ultra-runner and transcontinental record-keeper John Wallace III on the bible of transcontinental race data, www.usacrossers.com. Weston was seventy years old when he did it, going 3,895 miles from New York to San Francisco in 121.417 days, an average of 32.08 miles a day.

In fact, transcontinental attempts go back to the late 1800s. Accomplished runners and unprepared dreamers alike have tried and failed to reach the finish line, no less make it in record-breaking time. It is safe to say that another one hundred or so runners have cut their quest short since Frank Giannino set the world record in 1980.

But there has never had the influx of transcontinental adventures like those taking place now. There have been 175 documented crossings in the thirty-six years since Frank's record run. More notably, there have been 71 documented crossings since 2008, more than a quarter of the total.

Frank made two of the six recorded crossings in 1979 and 1980. By comparison, there were 36 documented crossings on record in 2011 and 2012.

Amid a record obesity rate and the greatest communication and video technological breakthroughs in American history, when youngsters and grownups alike are supposedly spending too much time inside peering at screens, why are so many people choosing to run across the United States of America?

"I'd like to think that people sort of end up wanting to give something back, so they do it for a cause," the great ultra-runner Marshall Ulrich said. "And I'd like to think it is people getting back to the basics of who they are, people who want to experience their geography, people who want to experience their homeland.

"What amazes me is that kids are doing it," Ulrich said. "They get a hold of me – eighteen- to twenty-four-year-olds – and go out and do it. It baffles me. I like it. I like that it's happening."

There is, for some, an innate desire to push their body to its limit. It is why the half-marathon (13.1 miles) and not the seemingly forever trendy 5K (3.1 miles) represented the fastest growing road race distance in the U.S. through 2008, according to *Running USA*. People like a challenge. And for most, the half-marathon and marathon distances represent an ample goal.

But three thousand miles? That comes out to 114½ marathons. That is when the field of eligible runners severely dwindles.

It is a skill set and mind set completely foreign to ninety-nine percent of the population. Many folks can't even fathom the endeavor, and articulating the brutality of the experience can be a challenge in itself, perhaps lending to cross country runs being largely unappreciated by the masses.

Frank certainly can appreciate the experience having twice run across America. Yet for 3½ decades, he has held a strong conviction regarding the record.

Frank is baffled that the record has stood up for so long. He has continually called himself a "no-talent ultra-marathoner" in reference to the unique breed of distance runners racing beyond the 26.2-mile marathon standard. In fact, Frank doesn't really consider running across the country an ultra-marathon. He calls it a survival/journey run, with the "ultra" part of the run representing ultra-slow running.

"I think a lot of people can do it if they put themselves out there to survive," Frank said. "I never doubted I could run fifty miles a day. But I knew I could fall apart in a fifty-mile race. I just knew I could run a slow pace for a long time. The difference between me and other guys is that people can go out and run a 9:30 (per-mile) pace all day. I can't do that. My fastest days were 11:30 and my slowest day was 14-flat. There are some ultra-marathoners who are not going to hold up for a long time because they would get hurt."

Frank insists the record is soft. Yet he has watched brilliant ultra-runners, many well-organized in their efforts, fail to erase the mark. "I think a lot of people can do it if they put themselves out there to survive," Frank said. "If I interviewed each runner attempting a transcontinental race, I could tell you which ones will make it and which ones won't."

Frank insists there is no hidden secret, no precious training tool or unconventional practice that allowed him to average 66.94 miles for forty-six days while totaling 3,103 miles from San Francisco to New York in 1980.

He cites five main factors necessary to have a shot at the record. None of them are unique to the gifted distance runner. Yet employing them collectively during one hundred percent of the run makes the task exceedingly difficult. Frank's factors:

- physical ability
- desire
- dedication
- mind set
- support (financial and logistical).

The physical. "I think a good ultra-marathoner has a better chance," Frank said. "I think it just comes down to the individual. Luck of the draw, genetics, how your body responds."

The desire. "You gotta' have desire," he said. "Not just the dream, but the desire."

You must not only commit to necessary planning and training. You must be passionate about it. You must look forward to almost every morsel of preparation geared toward the run. It should consume your life, if only temporarily, without ever becoming drudgery. Without one hundred percent desire, runners will be unprepared for the inevitable pitfalls that take place on the roads.

"What really excited me most was that I knew I could do it," Frank said. "I was inspired by the romance of West Coast/East Coast. You have to be ready to overcome any challenge."

The dedication. "You gotta' stay dedicated to the goal despite life's distractions," Frank said. "It's like trying to break the mile world record. It's not seconds, it's a tenth of a second. Every step you take toward it is for that goal."

Dedication is more a physical factor than desire. You must live for the run, plan and train for it full-time, log the miles while testing yourself against the elements. There must be no shortcuts in preparation.

The mind set. Frank was one hundred percent certain he would finish his runs despite a mountain of obstacles. In both runs, he faced major support issues, monetary and sponsorship problems and, of course, a relative lack of long-distance training. Yet by the time he left on his second run, Frank was convinced that he would break the world record. He buried shreds of doubt deep in his consciousness and refused to allow those particles of negativity to surface. When doubt and a lack of desire threatened to end his quest in Pennsylvania, Frank delved deep into his mind for the necessary strength.

The mind set also covers a need to break down every aspect of the trip mentally. "It's more than being a good runner," Frank said. "You gotta' know the setbacks that are going to come your way. Even the toughest guy in the world can wilt in the end. You must know your body inside and out.

"And patience with yourself, and never, ever give up. You have to be ready to overcome any challenge."

The support. "You have to be a good leader. You need money to pay for it, at least $25,000. You must have a great support team. Interrogate your support team. Ask why are you there? I had the innocence of great friends with Billy Glatz and Becky Wright) fresh out of college on the first run. To me, friendship and loyalty surpassed talent and qualifications. If I started today, I'd have a team of medical experts to monitor everything. If you don't have the right temperament and tolerance, you are not going to be able to work with other people. You have to be everything. Believe me, all of my crew were watching me. If I blinked, they would blink."

Still, from a technical standpoint, Frank would seem to have lacked the long-distance experience to break the record. He was a 2:30-something marathoner with almost no ultra-training. He did big weekly miles leading to the runs. He added a couple of adventure runs. But all in all, he did only a handful of workouts beyond the marathon distance.

Yet he was stubborn enough, even naïve enough, to believe that he could do it.

"I truly feel that in my life, I never quit on anything," Frank said. "I was fueled by emotions. Having family there was a key in the second run. I'm really disappointed that nobody that I know of, other than Marshall Ulrich, really wanted to break the record."

That might not be totally accurate. At least a couple runners per year typically reach out to Frank for guidance in trying to break his record. But it's almost impossible to determine how many of them set out believing one hundred percent that they are going to take down his mark.

Frank has watched from afar while becoming something of a consultant to dozens of cross-America hopefuls. The phone rings at his store or an e-mail arrives at his inbox from runners looking to pick his brain. How did you do it? What was your course? What kind of support team? Your run schedule? Injuries? Diet?

Frank has felt no obligation to conceal trade secrets, maybe because he doesn't have any. What Frank has been for the cross-country crowd is how he once described his dad – a friendly voice on the other end of the phone. And his message has been consistent through the years. It's a soft record, he tells the hopefuls. You can do it. I'm rooting for you. Let me know how I can help.

But why? Why would a man who spent half a lifetime searching for self-fulfillment and recognition and, finally, his ultimate running accomplishment, comfortably accept fading from the spotlight?

For all his relative anonymity holding the record, imagine the lack of recognition he would get if someone broke it.

Frank certainly feels a sense of enjoyment over the attention associated with the record. But that is only a small part of it. The way Frank sees it, he accomplished his goal and nothing will diminish his standing.

But Frank feels strongly about at least one aspect of his record: the course. In Frank's mind, supported by Ulrich, the course should run from San Francisco to New York. Frank is adamant that other cross-country courses are easier.

"I ran against Stan Cottrell's accomplishment from New York to San Francisco," Frank said. "It's the terrain."

***

But how exactly do runners go about proving they ran across the country at all, no less in a specific time?

What stops people from pulling a Rosie Ruiz, the infamous Cuban-American who literally and figuratively came from nowhere to win the 1980 Boston Marathon in a female race-record time of 2:31:56?

Ruiz, of course, was found to have cheated when she was missing from video footage and nobody could swear to seeing her at checkpoints throughout the race. Ruiz was disqualified later in the week.

What could keep cross-country runners from doing the same? Some trans-con runners take great measures to prove their run's authenticity. But despite the multiple steps involved in verification, cheaters just as determined as legitimate runners could get away with the feat much easier than, say, Ruiz did in 1980.

This is where things get particularly sticky because the run, in many ways, is conducted on the honor system.

There are detailed rules attached to having the feat sanctioned by Guinness World Records (GWR, as the organization calls itself).

And we are talking detailed rules, as in four thousand words worth of direction that weren't followed in its entirety by Frank for one simple reason – some of them include employing such measures as GPS, the tracking system that was decades from being invented when Frank ran.

Here is a sampling from the Guidelines to Guinness World Record Qualification:

1. The attempt should start at City Hall New York and finish at City Hall Los Angeles or San Francisco (or vice versa). The mileage covered is not relevant to the attempt – it is up to the participant to choose the most suitable or shortest route between these two points.

2. The run should only proceed on roads where it is safe and/or legal to run. The breaking of any laws during the journey will result in disqualification.

3. The record will be timed from the moment the runner sets off to the moment he/she arrives at their final destination. Breaks may be taken as desired, but at no time will the clock stop.

4. The runner is allowed the benefit of a support team, but at no time may he/she be transported towards his/her destination by the support vehicle. Each leg of the journey should resume at the exact point at which the last leg ended.

For the purposes of verifying any claim, the following must be provided:

WITNESS BOOK

Any attempt must take place in view of the public, wherever possible, and a book made available for independent witnesses to sign. The book should be set up so that the following details can be included for each potential witness:

Date & Time
Location
Name
Signature

For solo and unsupported attempts, we appreciate that it might not be possible to gain an unbroken line of witnesses for the attempt, but one should try to obtain as many as possible. For an attempt, which is supported by a backup team, we would expect it to be possible to gain sufficient numbers of independent witnesses to enable verification for the entire duration of the attempt. Where possible, local dignitaries and police should be sought to sign the book.

GENERAL 'PLACE TO PLACE' GUIDELINES

- The name of the organization, company or person(s) making the attempt must be given, along with the date and place.
- Details of how the distances have been calculated must be given before the attempt starts so the GWR can confirm these measurements are correct.
- Accurate professional equipment i.e. GPS equipment (and associated printout) must be used.
- The clock starts the moment the participant crosses the starting line and does not stop until they reach their goal.
- Note that no distinction will be made between supported and unsupported journeys.
- As a general rule, the participant should not remain stationary (i.e. if he/she does not make any progress towards his/her destination) for longer than 14 days. Any delays longer than this should have a very good reason (i.e. injury) and must be accounted for to Guinness World Records. Note that delays that cannot be reasonably justified may result in disqualification.
- All measurements must be given in both metric and imperial terms.

ADDITIONAL EVIDENCE

- GPS printout as requested above
- Witness Book
- Log Book

This book should give an adequate description of the event and full details of the participant(s) daily/overall performance.

It must be clear from the book the exact start and finish points of each leg of the attempt, the exact start and finish times and calculation of daily and total distances traveled.

All rest breaks or stoppages for whatever reason must also be fully detailed in the log. Failure to include the required documentation will ultimately delay the outcome of your claim or lead to its rejection.

As an additional form of verification, receipts for hotels, fuel, food etc. may be provided as proof of position on a particular day.

To attest to the validity and genuineness of the claim, we require signed statements of authentication by two independent persons of some standing, one of whom should have attended the beginning of the event, and if possible the end.

These statements should originate directly from the witnesses (in their own hand) and be submitted where possible on their own headed notepaper and include full contact details.

Statements should not take the form of documents pre-prepared by those involved in the record attempt.

There is more, much more, needed to satisfying Guinness. And for good reason. The very nature of such runs – long periods of isolation – lends itself to the prospect of cheating.

The packet of materials that must be turned in to Guinness includes:

- Cover letter
- Two witness statements or signed affidavit by a public notary
- Independent corroboration in the form of media coverage
- Video footage of the record attempt on VHS, DVD or CD ROM video
- High-quality color photographs
- Guideline-specific evidence: log books, official statements and measurements.

Guinness then details its requirements for the cover letter and witness statements. The witness statements section is particularly intricate. For example:

Preferably, the witnesses must have 'standing' in the local community, meaning that they must be prominent and respected. Examples of such persons include: Justices of the

Peace; police officers; judges; mayors or town councilors; Members of Parliament; doctors; ordained ministers of religion; newspaper editors etc. We understand that this is not always possible (especially in the case of endurance marathons), so we would accept statements *so long as the witnesses are truly independent.* (See below).

Except where both the witnesses are members of the same professional body, or are officials of a national sporting organization (or similar), the witnesses must be independent of each other as well as independent of the person(s) attempting the record. *Independent means that they are not normally associated with, or related to, the record organisers or participants, nor have anything to gain from the attempt* e.g. bar owners where the event is taking place would not be deemed 'independent' as they have something to gain from the publicity of the record.

In other words, Frank had to have been grandfathered in. As if breaking Frank's record isn't daunting enough, current record-chasers have their work cut out trying to meet the sanctioning requirements.

Frank failed to satisfy the criteria in many areas, namely supplying "independent witnesses not normally associated with, or related to, the record organiser or participants, nor have anything to gain from the attempt; i.e. bar owners where the event is taking place would not be deemed 'independent' as they have something to gain from the publicity of the record."

Frank's independent witnesses, other than early departing public relations member Bruce Goldberg, were relatives: his father, brother and step-mom.

Frank left from San Francisco City Hall but failed to finish at New York City Hall. Frank's record-breaking finish line was on the toll booth of the Verrazano-Narrows Bridge connecting Staten Island with Brooklyn, famous as the starting line for the New York City Marathon. He fulfilled sponsor obligations with a ceremonial finish the following day nearby on the Brooklyn Bridge, and afterward walked the half mile to City Hall for a brief news conference.

Frank couldn't remember if he included a City Hall-to-City Hall blueprint as part of detailed paperwork sent to Guinness after the run. He foresaw no problems once Guinness verified the record and documented the mark in its publications over the years. But Frank realized all these years later that his finish-line location could be questioned.

Frank, after all, didn't figure on owning the record his entire life. He has gotten genuinely excited when sensing the emergence of a true threat to his record.

***

Never was Frank as pumped for a record-breaking attempt as the day in 2008 – Feb. 13 to be exact – when a five-sentence note popped into his e-mail:

Subject: Trans Con
Frank,
My name is Charlie Engle. Last year I became the first person (with 2 co-runners) to run all the way across the Sahara Desert. I would like to talk to you about your Trans Con record if you are willing. I will explain when we talk. Thanks.
Charlie Engle

Frank ran a quick Internet search and concluded that here was the guy to break his record. Frank's confidence in Engle rose even further when he learned that he would be joined on the run that September by Ulrich – one of the best ultra-marathoners in history.

Their high-profile presence and keen interest in breaking Frank's standard reminded Frank of his own legacy. And maybe Ulrich and Engle, regardless of whether they broke the record, would provide Frank with a final round of applause and accolades as he approached retirement age. The runners planned to recognize Frank's accomplishment along the way through media interviews and a documentary film being produced of the run. As far as Frank was concerned, it would be a record-breaking run. These guys had the credentials to do it.

The timing was ideal for Frank. He was having major financial problems with his business, Frank's Shoe-Fitting, two years after opening the larger store. Frank needed a pick-me-up in the worst way. He needed to feel worthy again.

"Marshall and Charlie effectively forced me to look back at my runs with more clarity," Frank said. "Because they were using my model, that was huge. They were taking my advice. I began to change everything I was doing in my business to thinking about what was important to me."

And these guys certainly were inspiring.

Engle, born in North Carolina, was approaching his forty-sixth birthday. In 2007, Engle and two teammates had become the first people to run 4,500 miles across the entire Sahara Desert. Engle averaged forty-two miles a day for one hundred and eleven straight days in some of the most hellish conditions on Earth.

Engle had marked a significant date on his Web site – July 23, 1992 – his sobriety birthday after ten years of abusing drugs and alcohol. He had become a TV producer, having helped create more than thirty episodes of ABC's *Extreme Makeover Home Edition.*

Ulrich, born in Colorado, has accomplished one seemingly impossible task after another. His only liability appeared to be his age, fifty-seven. But Ulrich once ran five days to finish a 457-mile race after venom from a rattlesnake bite caused immediate leg swelling and semi-consciousness. He crossed Death Valley on foot a record twenty-four times and climbed Mount Everest. He was best known for running the Badwater Ultramarathon, a 135-mile midsummer race from the bottom of Death Valley (282 feet below sea level amid triple-digit temperatures) to the top of Mount Whitney (at 14,495 feet, the highest point in the lower forty-eight states). His Badwater training included running in place ... in a sauna. He avoided the common distance-running problem of blackened toenails by having them surgically removed.

"Suffering," Ulrich liked to say, "is a learned behavior."

Now they were going to take down Frank's record. And Frank, who needed six thousand miles of foot patrol to reach running fulfillment, was going to do everything he could to help them.

Frank and the runners exchanged e-mails and calls over the ensuing months. He laid out his course for them. He stressed the importance of a reliable support staff. He told them to be flexible, to free themselves from their itinerary when necessary, and to be patient. They planned to reach out to Frank during the run, to use him as a lifeline, as Engle put it.

While the respective resumes of Ulrich and Engle were filled with awe-inspiring feats, Frank's accolades essentially consisted of two amazing three thousand-mile runs. He had finished only eleven marathons and a few forty- and fifty-mile training runs, small potatoes in the ultra-world, before running across the country for the first time in 1979. Despite owning the record, Frank, who referred to himself as the no-talent ultra-marathoner, felt a bit out of place as a hero to two of the top ultra-runners on the planet.

Engle and Ulrich were moved by Frank's humility and generosity. They would follow about ninety-five percent of his course and one hundred percent of his advice. "The five percent of the course we don't use," Engle said, "is because it doesn't exist anymore"

"Part of my focus is honoring people like Frank who came before us," Ulrich said less than forty-eight hours before setting out on the run. "He's just an extraordinary human being. One of the things that struck me about Frank was that he was so generous and willing to offer up information. He offered some of the best ideas. 'Don't try to stick to any schedule,' he told us. It sounds like he operated from the seat of his pants, and that's what I like. Another thing Frank said in his e-mails was that the crew was going to be the key."

Ulrich added, "This is the last thing on my to-do list. Some people are afraid of success. To me, I'm afraid of failure."

Days before the run, Engle said, "I could only hope I could ever handle this situation as gracefully as Frank. One of the things I talked about with Marshall was, if we fail to break the record or succeed, it's going to bring deserved attention to Frank. Not that Frank cares, but it's such an astounding record, including the fact that he ran it two years in a row."

Frank's bond with Ulrich and Engle felt deeper than even the trio's steely will and sense of adventure. Frank's mom and sister had both died of breast cancer. Ulrich started running in 1979 – about the time Giannino made his first cross-country trek – to help curb his own high blood pressure after first wife was diagnosed with breast cancer. She died two years later at age thirty.

All three of them had been divorced, with Ulrich on his fourth marriage. Giannino had two children from his first marriage and two step-children. Ulrich had three children, one from his first wife and two from his second wife. Engle had two teen boys at the time of the run.

On Sept. 13, 2008, Engle and Ulrich took off from San Francisco, each with an RV and four-person support teams. Of course, Engle and Ulrich had a fifth person on their team. He was three thousand miles and a phone call away.

From: frankg@shoe-fitter.com
Sent: Sunday, August 31, 2008 1:14 PM
To: Marshall Ulrich; Charlie Engle
Marshall & Charlie:
I truly wish both of you the best on September 13th. My head and my heart will be with you as you pursue each day's goal coming across America. I know "first hand" of the incredible amount of pressure, and "patience" that will definitely be required, in order for both of you to stay on pace, especially together. Having thoroughly read your stories, I truly feel, for the first time in 28 years, that "you two are the ones" that have the ability to do 70+ miles per day, maybe even more. I wouldn't let an "itinerary" hold you back if things are clicking out there.

Reflecting back to 1980, my "low day" was 46 miles; the "high day" was 82 miles. I "cherished" the "alone time" in the breakdown lane and on the road shoulder. I "loved" the attention along the way, but did not enjoy too much of it, as I felt it took too much away from the emotional part of my effort.

I am frequently asked why people do these kinds of things. I answer with one word: "ownership." All of us have a burning desire to "own" something, even if it is as simple as an endurance achievement. Once you have reached your goal, you

*"own" that accomplishment, and can savor it for a lifetime. No
one can ever take away from you the intrinsic satisfaction that
comes from the completion of a goal. And of course, we keep on
setting them.*
   You both "inspire the already inspired."
   Never stop running and "never, ever give up."
   If there is anything you both need, call anytime.
   Best of luck!
   Frank Giannino
   1979 and 1980 USA Transcontinental Runner

What Ulrich and Engle needed, or at least could have used,
were each other. They seemingly had the variables necessary to
break the record. They were elite ultra-marathoners with piles of
experience in adverse situations. They had the financial means to
afford top-notch support teams, including a doctor on hand. They
had a detailed analysis of Frank's runs.

But there is no foolproof blueprint for running across
America. It's not a 10K in which you hit your splits and gut it out
to the finish. At some point during a run across the country,
often early on, you dig deeply every single day for hours on end.
You run through excruciating pain. You try to fix pain and
injuries and hope they pass.

"I originally thought about, 'Can I break Frank's record?'"
Ulrich said. "I came to the conclusion that I was going to put
myself out there. I wanted to break the grand masters (fifty-and-
older) record and the master's record (forty-and-older). But to
break Frank's record, I would have had to have everything work
absolutely perfectly."

Bad omens abounded from the start. Only days before they
were set to take off, Engle got his first cold in years. It cost him
much-needed rest leading to the run. Ulrich, as he would
chronicle in his fascinating book *Running On Empty* felt like he
was in a foot race with Engle from the start.

Both paid a steep price. Engle made it about one-third of the
way before dropping out with a leg injury. Ulrich got plantar
fasciitis in his right foot in Utah, 2,500 miles from the finish line.
His crew, including wife Heather, believed the run was over.

"None of us said it out loud," Heather said, "but we thought, 'This is it.'"

Marshall ran through the injury. He suffered a lateral tear in a tendon in the same foot in Colorado and endured that for some two thousand miles. He slightly dislocated his left tibia and suffered an infection, requiring antibiotics, from one of his blisters formed during the run. He suffered from severe pain in the knees, ankles, Achilles' and back. Heather Ulrich said her husband also suffered from horrific sleep deprivation and loneliness during the run.

He was almost hit by a car. Somebody took a shot at him.

"I think the biggest thing people ask me is, 'What was the hardest part?'" Heather Ulrich said. "For me, the hardest part was watching someone I love that much suffer that much. So many times Marshall was in tears, he was so miserable. I wanted to shake him and say, 'THEN QUIT!' There were so many times I wanted to tell him to quit. But you can't do it."

Running so many miles with plantar fasciitis took an enormous toll on Ulrich's body. Even eight months later, as he stepped to the starting line with eyes toward finishing another Badwater, Ulrich had a golf-ball sized knot of scar tissue on the right foot. Still jarred physically and emotionally from the cross-country run, he had barely been able to train for Badwater. Less than halfway into the race, Heather made a suggestion to her husband that she had never made before. She looked at him walking in Crocs, the only footwear tolerable given the intense pain radiating up and down his body, and said finally, "You need to stop."

Ulrich listened and dropped out.

But first came the evening of Nov. 4, 2008, an historic day in American history, when Marshall Ulrich's cross-country run neared the finish line at City Hall in New York City.

With the U.S. about to introduce its first black president, Barack Obama, Ulrich ran down Broadway Street in Manhattan a little past seven p.m., his entire rooting section amounting to eight runners who had joined him on his final leg.

One was Todd Jennings, a forty-six-year-old Hudson Valley resident and friend of Frank's, who had received a random e-mail seven months earlier. The note asked if he was interested in running a mile with Engle and Ulrich, which to a running nut like Jennings represented a can't-miss opportunity. In July, Jennings learned he had been chosen to run with the pair in New York City.

The one-mile rule originally floated by organizers was just a number, as it turned out. Jennings wound up running twelve miles with Ulrich. Jennings and fellow pacers took turns running up front with Ulrich, who was sandwiched by a support vehicle and film-crew vehicle serving as buffers through one of the busiest streets in America. Ulrich and his team remarkably managed to navigate the traffic without being side-swiped by any of the city's legendary cabbies.

"The thing that still strikes me, and will for the rest of my life," Jennings said, "is that he ran right through Times Square at six-thirty at night. Not on the side of the street – right through the middle of the street!"

There was only one thing more amazing than Ulrich's run. The reception. There was even less fanfare than for Frank's finishes three decades earlier. Ulrich had no police escort, no sirens blaring or cops on motorcycles leading the way, only wise-guys occasionally jumping off sidewalks to briefly join in the run. The support team was down to a van holding Heather and another support-staff person, a four-person documentary film crew, four runners helping pace the final miles and a few family members and friends. In all, thirty people witnessed the end to one of the most amazing athletic achievements in sport.

Ulrich stopped a block from City Hall to change into his finisher's T-shirt. Cops inside a booth opened the automated black steel gates and Ulrich turned left to head for the finish near the steps of City Hall.

Only a few more steps remained. A half-dozen people waited, a freelance photographer, a few acquaintances, a reporter and a couple who had made the ninety-minute drive from an Orange County, New York, store. They had never met Ulrich in person, but they were among the first people to arrive at City Hall ninety minutes before his finish.

Michele and Frank Giannino.

Ulrich walked up the long steps and tossed his hat in the air at the top. He embraced Heather, who intermittently sobbed and laughed, the emotions from her husband's feat flowing fast. Ulrich finished his 3,063-mile run from San Francisco in 52.50 days, averaging almost 58.35 miles a day. He would claim cross-country records in both the masters and grand masters divisions.

Frank's world record of averaging 66.94 miles for forty-six days, however, was safe.

"Any time I talked to Frank, he wanted to give me tips and pointers," Ulrich said. "I cannot tell you how incredible that was to me. To me, it was like the President of the United States greeting me, and it really brought home the magnitude of what he had done."

Though Frank had arrived an hour and a half earlier, he had joined Ulrich spiritually all the way from the start in San Francisco. They had become fast friends. Their bond was the Run Across America.

Ulrich walked to the bottom steps of City Hall with Heather as cameras flashed. "Where's Frank?" he asked. "Where's Frank?"

Frank stood a few feet away quietly watching the scene unfold. He stepped forward. They shook hands. They hugged.

"You are the man!" Ulrich told Giannino. "You are the man!"

"No," Frank said, "you are."

Ulrich, who had climbed the highest mountain in every continent, who had performed all kinds of crazy endurance runs, once again found himself in awe of the fifty-six-year-old store owner reduced to sporadic three-mile jogs.

"I cannot believe what you did!" Ulrich told Frank. "I am amazed. I thought about you out there and I thought, 'How the hell did you do that?' I'm so humbled. I'm so humbled to meet you."

They talked for several more minutes as the film crew took footage. "Well, the fun's over," Ulrich said. "Tell me what I'm in for."

Frank told Ulrich about his own euphoric rush crashing into a depression that kept him inside for at least three days. They talked some more and somebody handed each of them a cup of champagne.

"Cheers!" Ulrich said.

"Cheers!" Giannino said.

Pressed on the ride back home, Frank admitted, "A little bit of me was happy that he hadn't broken it. But I was more curious to meet him and see how he felt when he was done. Something happens to people who are out there week after week."

"It's not like an adrenaline rush," Heather Ulrich said. "You are out there so long, the adrenaline is gone. And to do this two years in a row as Frank did, I can't imagine the focus and drive to go out there and do it again. People say, 'Will you try it again?' and Marshall says, 'Hell no!' Frank is Marshall's hero."

***

A year after Marshall finished the run, Frank received correspondence from Geoff Weber, a former nationally ranked cyclist turned long-distance runner. Weber had been overweight and unable to run a mile as recently as 1998 before turning himself into an accomplished ultra-marathoner. Weber was Marine tough, participating in more than one thousand runs and other athletic events.

He made the *Guinness Book of World Records* for fastest 50K on a treadmill and then broke his own record, first setting the mark of 3:46:12 aboard a Navy ship and breaking it at a sports convention in Las Vegas.

He was home from deployment as a Navy officer when he planned to break his 50K record and set new fifty-mile and 100K records in less than eight hours. Alas, leg cramps and problems in his calves and hamstrings cost him shots at those records. He finished more than thirteen minutes slower than his own 50K record.

"Sometimes," Weber said afterward, "you're the windshield and sometimes you're the bug."

On Nov. 1, 2006, Weber completed the 262-mile Run Across Virginia for the American Lung Association, running on average fifty-five miles for four days while a friend drove an RV for support. He ran the Marine Corps Marathon in Washington, D.C., in 2006, and then jogged the 209 miles home to Virginia

Beach to average fifty-five miles for three days. That was about the time Weber decided to run across the United States.

But averaging fifty-five miles for a few days was one thing. Averaging sixty-something miles for forty-something days was quite another.

Still, Weber carried on, spending four years working on the logistics of the run, from choosing the route to, eventually, getting the time off from work. Weber's training involved about two hundred miles a week. He jogged to and from work during the week, about twenty-eight miles a day, and did double-session twenty-milers on both Saturday and Sunday.

In November 2009, Weber typed an email to Frank:

From: Geoff Weber
Sent: Monday, November 02, 2009 8:19 p.m.
To: frank@shoe-fitter.com
Subject: Transcontinental Run

Mr. Giannino,
I'm an endurance runner and have dreamed of running across America for many years. My goal is to run (largely unsupported) from LA to NY with a Camelbak, Smartphone and a credit card. The military may afford me this opportunity next year. I feel driven to take this journey, but not for any particular cause.

A very presumptuous promotional video, but explains some of my background: www.youtube.com/watch?v=uiR7n9bmMTg

As the current record holder, I'm sure you receive a few emails every year from people like me who ask if you have any advice. Some of us may even fascinate it's possible to break your record and complete the run in under 46 days. I have great respect for what you've done and would really appreciate asking you a few questions.

Might I have a 30-minute telephone discussion with you one day? If so, please reply with your number and a time that it's suitable for me to call you.
Very respectfully,
LT Geoff Weber, USN

Confidence was hardly a factor. Weber posted a video on his Web site proclaiming plans to break the record. Frank had indeed come away from conversations with Weber thinking he might have a shot at it.

Weber used Google Earth to study much of his route, previewing locations of motels and restaurants along the way. He planned to awake each day at three a.m. by means of wake-up calls from members of his church group, and run about eight to sixteen hours with as-needed breaks. Followers could keep an eye on Weber's run on Facebook or on his Web site.

Weber would carry a nine-pound pack that included the eighty-ounce Camelbak (a device used to carry water), a cell phone, a hand-held GPS and a credit card. He would follow a nine-thousand-calorie daily diet.

"I intend to live off the American roadside terrain," Weber said. "This includes fast-food restaurants, public restrooms, post offices and sleeping at motels along the route. I'll have a few packages with consumables sent in advance to scheduled stops, including toiletries, detergent, and new shoes."

Weber, a forty-two-year-old husband and father of three, set out from the Santa Monica Pier – destination Battery Park in New York City – on April 23, 2010. Like Giannino, Weber dipped a foot in the Pacific Ocean as he departed from California. Unlike Giannino, Weber never made it to the Atlantic side.

Three days later, Weber quit his run. His note on Facebook read, "There were just not enough locations for drinking water on the remainder of the route to support this level of activity. Sadly, the roads of America are no safe place for a simple man on foot."

Frank could relate, remembering concerns over a lack of available water during points of his runs. "He was enthusiastic," Frank said. "I don't know why he blew up."

Actually Frank had a pretty good idea why Weber failed. He ran without a support team, virtually guaranteeing a premature and dismal end to his run. Weber's decision to lug a pack was similar to the plan concocted by Billy Glatz, Frank's running partner in his first trek across America, before Frank talked Glatz into allowing support.

"People say to me, 'I want to break Frank's record' – at least four people, maybe more," Ulrich said. "Well, you go right ahead and give it your best shot."

Ulrich has tried to share with record-breaking hopefuls the otherworldly nature of Frank's mark. But he often gets the feeling that, "Holy shit, you have no idea."

That is because nobody has any idea until they try it. The most difficult aspect of advising others about a transcontinental run is vividly relaying the near insurmountable pain and anguish necessary to reach the finish line.

***

Ulrich added to his list of achievements in August 2012 when, at age sixty-one, he finished an unprecedented expedition around the entire perimeter of Death Valley National Park during the hottest part of summer.

Ulrich and firefighter Dave Heckman completed 425 miles in sixteen days completely unaided and unassisted, having buried water, food and supplies along the route two months earlier. They crossed six mountain ranges with a total of about forty thousand feet of elevation gain as temperatures exceeded 120 degrees.

Yet for all of Ulrich's brow-raising achievements, he doesn't hesitate when asked his greatest accomplishment – running across the United States.

"Because every day you have to do relentless mileage," said Ulrich, who averaged just more than fifty-eight miles a day for 52½ days covering 3,063 miles. "It's so darn much harder. You approach sixty miles a day or past sixty miles – that puts it in a whole other ballpark. There are a rare few who can even entertain coming close to that. You need the perfect blend of desire, durability and mental strength."

Runners have approached Ulrich for advice and tips on trying to break the record. The first question he asks is, what is your marathon time? Ulrich's 26.2-mile personal best is just under three hours.

"Speed does translate into the ability to break the record," he said. "You have to be fast enough to move fast enough so that you will have enough down time to recover. If they are not able to run at least a three-hour marathon, I question whether they can even do it.

"The hills and everything; having to dodge cars; wind; the elements – that all takes it to a whole other level. Some of them don't have the credentials."

Ulrich mentioned two runners with a shot at breaking Frank's record should they make the attempt. One is Floridian Mike Morton, who won all five races he entered in 2012, including coming within just more than a minute of breaking the Badwater course record.

The other is Scott Jurek of Boulder, Colorado, who has won almost every elite ultra-marathon. In 2010, Jurek set a U.S. all-surface record in the 24-Hour Run by completing 165.7 miles, 6.5 marathons in a single day.

Ulrich and Frank also have great respect for Connie Gardner, a forty-nine-year-old resident of Medina, Ohio. In September 2012, Gardner and Morton set 24-hour women's and men's American records. Morton ran 172.5 miles to break Jurek's mark and Gardner finished 149.4 miles to erase Sabrina Moran's record of 148.4.

British athlete Dr. Lizzy Hawker holds the women's 24-hour world record, having completed 153.5 miles in September 2011 at the Commonwealth Ultra Championship in Llandudno, North Wales.

Ulrich deemed it possible for a woman to break Frank's record, but, as he put in his Dreams in Action blog, "I wonder if anyone else will attempt it. It's pretty much a no-glory, costly undertaking, so I'm curious to see if there will be any world-class athlete who will make another attempt."

Gardner, in fact, had set her sights on breaking Frank's record and talked of planning an attempt. Frank, for one, thinks she can do it. And once again, Frank claimed he would have no problem handing off the record.

"I'd feel happy for her," he said. "I have a lot of respect for her as a runner. She has the speed and the ability to endure. She ran 149 miles in 24 hours. She ran a 9:30 per-mile pace!"

Said Ulrich, "I think, yes, there are people out there who could do it on a physical level. But you have the durability factor and the mental part."

So the world record for fastest transcontinental run continues to be held by a man who choked in big meets as a kid, a former marathoner with no ultra background, a guy who has spent most of his sixty-four years searching for acceptance and adulation. The record is Frank Giannino's.

For now.

Frank and Marshall toast one another at City Hall, New York City, at the end of Marshall's cross-country run.

21

On the Road to Recovery

Frank had an extra hop to his step on a late April day in 2011. He left the store to his trusted assistant and headed ninety minutes southeast to Manhattan with Michele. Marshall Ulrich had invited Frank to the launch of his book, *Running on Empty*, chronicling his spirited run at Frank's world record in 2008.

They had become good friends, keeping in close contact since Ulrich started planning his run and corresponding during the run. Frank had grown quite fond of Marshall, and it meant a lot to him when Marshall demanded his presence at the launch.

Frank had wanted to be among the first people to congratulate Marshall at the finish line. Now he wanted to be one of the first people inside Gary Muhrcke's running store on 49th and 7th to celebrate Marsh's night.

There were whispers about the room as Frank mingled inside the store. "That's the guy who holds the world record. That's the guy I was telling you about." Marshall, with typical humility, warmly introduced Frank to folks in attendance as the guy whose record still stood.

"From the time I hit Colorado, I was in work mode," Frank told somebody before the festivities. "I was beginning to have the worst pain – abdominal – because I was getting used to breathing heavier for so long. But Marshall had injury pain – that's a big difference."

Ulrich had long carved a successful business career. Now he had proven that he could be part of a riveting book as well, delivering a wonderfully vivid account of his run. But Ulrich wasn't the only ultra-successful man in the room to benefit greatly through running. In Ulrich's case, he used his business acumen to help spur his running career. In Muhrcke's case, he used his running career to catapult his business career.

Muhrcke was an accomplished marathoner when he reached into his pocket for the $1 fee and entered the first New York City Marathon on an eighty-five-degree day in September 1970. He steered around four loops of Central Park to beat 126 competitors in 2:31:38. A fireman, Muhrcke soon started selling shoes out of his van, the same method Frank had used in his early business days. By 1978, Muhrcke had opened two running stores. Muhrcke opened the first New Balance store in June 1995 and built an operation that included eleven stores and one hundred employees in and around New York City.

Ulrich took the floor in front of several dozen people. He talked about the power of the human spirit. Ulrich amazingly had run thousands of miles with plantar fasciitis in his right foot, then continued with a lateral tear in a tendon in the same foot. While Ulrich hadn't known at the time, a doctor tending to him had given him only a thirty percent chance of finishing the run. Ulrich knew that a lot of people were counting him down and out, but he knew himself better than that. So he disowned his foot in order to keep going.

"That foot is not mine," he told the audience, sharing the conversation he had with wife Heather during the crossing. "It isn't who I am. It isn't my foot anymore."

It allowed Ulrich to take the focus off the foot. The next day he walked fifty miles. He pretty much maintained sixty- to sixty-two-mile days after that.

"You can do way, way more than you think you can," he told the crowd that night. "I was fifty-seven years old when I ran across the U.S. That's the point – never stop doing it. I grew up a country boy. I worked on a farm. I was not anything special. I was no different than you are. I just think I had a passion and that's what I identified with. When I was five years old, I decided I wanted to climb Mount Everest. I didn't get around to doing it 'til I was fifty-two years old, but I did get around to doing it. The only limitations are in your mind. If you don't think you can do it, you probably can't.

"People have asked me, 'Did you ever think about quitting?' I wanted to quit six or twelve times a day. It didn't really dawn on me until the end that I could make it."

Ulrich introduced Frank to the audience. "He is still the king of the road," Ulrich said. "That record has stayed for thirty-one years now."

Frank's new business plan was taking shape. He would never own a bunch of stores in the metropolitan New York area like Muhrcke, never enjoy the monetary benefits of his running career like Ulrich. But things were looking up.

Frank started to make money again in 2012, averaging $1,500 in daily sales at his modest store down the road. In late 2012, he got a $15,000 loan to help pay off remaining debt and figured to have the loan paid in seven months. He had come a long way since sales plummeted to $320,000 in 2009, his final year in the larger store. Frank grew the business to $355,000 in his first year in the smaller store, 2010-11, and was on pace to do $450,000 in 2011-12.

"This next decade is going to be a great decade," Frank said, "because we are going to travel."

Other than spending a week together in Falmouth during the summer of 2011, Michele and Frank had done little traveling in years. They talked about spending a couple of weeks island hopping in Hawaii in the summer of 2013. Instead, they used the $10,000 set aside for the trip toward converting their finished basement into a full-blown apartment for Frank's daughter Caitlin and her husband. The couple would live with modest overhead while Caitlin finished graduate school at SUNY New Paltz.

Michele and Frank invested some money in a double-apartment time share in Florida not far from Michele's children. Hawaii was postponed to 2016, with a trip to Italy planned for 2017.

"These trips are just beginning," Frank said. "In our first period together, I was all about her. "The (large) building pulled me in. It was the biggest mistake of my life."

He planned to get back into the running community by directing and attending local races. He even figured to return to his sales roots by selling shoes out of his van at the races. Frank had found a comfortable place in life. He had walked his oldest daughter down the aisle. His business was thriving again. He was intent on taking breathers from work to see more of the world with Michele.

But Frank Giannino has been no stranger to conflict. Crises have emerged throughout his life, whether on foot or not, often with the finish line virtually in sight.

Soon he would feel both the warmth of acknowledgement and the disappointment of rejection. Frank's record suddenly seemed in jeopardy of being eliminated, not by another runner but by the very body that sanctioned it more than three decades earlier – the Guinness Book of World Records.

Frank and Michele.

22

Documenting the Record

In July 2012, a phone call brought Frank back to his record-breaking run thirty-two years earlier. On the line was Dave Klink, vice president of operations for a film company called Lucky Coffee Productions. Lucky Coffee had been started recently by filmmaker Brian Kalata, who wrote the critically acclaimed *Dinner Rush* and served as a location manager for network television productions and feature films.

Kalata's group wanted to produce a documentary film on distance-runner Dan Isaacson's attempt at breaking Frank's record. The run was tentatively set for Fall 2013, and the documentary would include Frank's back story as a point of reference, highlighting his challenges in the age of phone booths and TripTiks. Academy Award-winning producer Lynn Appelle would be among those assisting on the project.

Klink explained the story as centering on Isaacson's "reverence for you and your record." The company planned to produce a detailed look at the runners and their passion for doing something extraordinary. They were still ironing out details of the run, such as whether Isaacson would follow a route similar to Frank's or an entirely different path.

Either way, the idea was to acknowledge Frank's record while giving viewers an intimate look at the immense challenges of running across the country. Klink explained this in an e-mail to Frank:

I want to make something very clear. Dan is in no way,
shape, or form under the impression he is even in the same class
of runner you are. In fact, he says if he breaks the record it
should (and probably will) have an asterisk. He claims (and I
have no reason to doubt this assertion) your exact route under
exact conditions is nearly impossible to duplicate. WE WANT TO
MAKE THAT EVIDENT TO ALL. This dichotomy is what sets up
the pitch (led by you and Dan) to develop a regular (whether it
be every 4 years, 2 years, whatever) Trans-Con run. This is
going to be a great project which will really galvanize the
running community and draw everyone to the same conclusion:
We need a race that determines the best runner, regardless of
distance.

Frank was thrilled to hear about the documentary and the
potential for a large-scale transcontinental run. He had proposed
just such an event two months before leaving for his record-
setting run in 1980, penning a letter to The Athletics Congress,
precursor to USA Track & Field, the country's governing body
for running and race walking. Frank had written a two-page,
typed letter on 14-by-8½-inch paper:

My immediate concern is that if Athletics Congress
recognizes my run this fall, it will invite the rest of the good
ultra-marathoners and distance enthusiasts in the world to
gather once a year for a transcontinental race across the U.S.
from San Francisco City Hall to New York City Hall, In short, it
has been a dream of mine to see an annual transcontinental race
across the U.S. We could call it the Superthon. I'm proposing the
route be certified by bicycle and eventually build a reputation for
itself. If properly promoted, it could become a premier event –
Calendar Event – each year.
Having done this type of run once, I know the logistics
involved in producing such an event. By putting prize money up
as an incentive, this event would not only promote running, but it
would promote professionalism on the part of the athlete, which
would continue to help the direction of Athletics Congress.

Frank went on to detail his idea before signing off: *Dedicated to fitness and longevity through Running, Frank Giannino.*

Frank's idea had a deep history. But there have often been at least two consistent themes with cross-America runs: accuracy of claims and skepticism by ultra-runners, that unique group of runners competing at distances beyond the 26.2-mile marathon. Frank experienced such skepticism first-hand, having heard rumblings over the years questioning the veracity of his record.

The Transcontinental Footrace of 1928 was the first organized race across the country, traversing 3,400 miles from Los Angeles to New York City. It was the creation of promoter Charles C. Pyle, known as the P.T. Barnum of Professional Sports.

Pyle put together a field of about two hundred, with an entry fee a whopping $125, and used his promotional savvy to gain sponsorship and drum up media coverage. The winner took home $25,000, followed by $10,000 for the runner-up, $5,000 for third place, $2,500 for fourth and $1,000 each for the fifth-through tenth-place finishers. Much of the route was along spanking new Route 66.

Runners started at the same time and had to reach designated checkpoints. Each runner's time was clocked daily, and those failing to reach the checkpoint by midnight were disqualified. The winner had the fastest cumulative time.

Ever-skeptical reporters wearily called it the Bunion Derby.

More than half the runners dropped out by Day Three, and Pyle lost a fortune on the race. But it went off with Andy Payne, a twenty-year-old Cherokee Indian from Oklahoma, crossing the finish line at Madison Square Garden and credited with needing just 573 hours, 4 minutes, 34 seconds of running. Payne died in 1977, but he is remembered with the running of Oklahoma City's Andy Payne Memorial Marathon, which held its thirty-eighth edition in 2015.

Fifty-five runners crossed the finish line of the Bunion Race. John H. Wallace III, who authors the popular Web site usacrossers.com, a comprehensive yet incomplete listing of trans-con finishers, lists those fifty-five runners with identical averages of 41.6 miles per day.

The Bunion Derby was run again the next year, a 3,685-mile event from New York to Los Angeles. New Jersey policeman John Salo won the race in seventy-eight days to beat Englishman Peter Gavuzzi by three minutes. Salo earned $35,000 for his efforts.

A *Running Times* story noted that in the half-century following the Bunion races, a "number of solo runs across the continent have been made, but no organized race has taken place – possibly because of the extraordinary costs of participation made such an undertaking prohibitive to serious competitors without the incentive of large cash prizes."

The magazine also pointed to the failed attempt in 1982 by New York promoter Gene Schoor organizing the Transcontinental Marathon from Beverly Hills, California, to New York City, which apparently included a whopping $6 million in prize money and a winner's share of up to $500,000. It was to be limited to two hundred runners chosen on the basis of past performances in marathons and other long-distance races.

A year later, again according to *Running Times*, a similar plan for a coast-to-coast race sponsored by Converse shoes went undeveloped.

The Sea to Shining Sea Marathon seemed to be the most organized of transcontinental races. Set for Sept. 3, 1984, it would cover twelve states and three thousand miles from Runnemede, New Jersey, near Atlantic City, to Pasadena, California, while coinciding with the end of the Olympic Games in Los Angeles. The purse would total $3 million, with entry fees of $1,000 for individuals and $1,500 for eight-person teams. The individual winner would net $150,000 and the winning team $250,000.

Organizer Barry Ward, an Albuquerque, New Mexico, attorney, called it "an idea whose time has come" and "the world's ultimate marathon foot race." The field would be capped at five thousand. "This will be the biggest marathon ever, not only in terms of money but in magnitude and depth of emotions," Ward said in a press release. "It will be THE biggest sporting event in this country."

Ward believed others had failed in the endeavor by trying to secure big-money sponsorship. "We have reversed that," he said. "We are going to the runners first and let the sponsors come to us."

But by late February 1984, just 546 runners had requested entry into the event, and the race was moved to April 6, 1985, because of "certain logistical problems on the West Coast which we will be unable to solve by Sept. 3, and the fact that the purse is not yet guaranteed (and we will not run the Sea to Shining Sea Marathon until the $3 million purse is guaranteed)."

The race never went off.

So while there is significant history to the tran-con, there remains no modern-day certified event. The latest idea would be to pit the top ultra-marathoners in the world facing off amid a well-organized professionally run three thousand-mile road race.

Klink and Kalata, the filmmakers, wanted to get the ball rolling by shadowing Isaacson. And he was no ordinary fellow.

A native of Oregon, Isaacson was a University of Oregon freshman running the mile in 1999 when he suddenly collapsed a quarter-mile from the finish line. He awoke in a hospital with a dangerous lack of oxygen. Isaacson endured six months of tests. He finally met up with a specialist who looked at Isaacson's elongated fingers and tiny wrists. The doctor asked Isaacson to form a circle with his middle finger touching the tip of his thumb, then wrap the two fingers around an opposite wrist.

A typical person's fingers barely touch one another around the wrist. Isaacson's middle finger, however, reached all the way to the knuckle of his thumb.

"I bet you have Marfan syndrome," the doctor said.

Isaacson was called into the doctor's office after further tests. He, indeed, had Marfan syndrome, an inherited disorder that affects connective tissue. The syndrome may disrupt development and function in several sites, most commonly in the heart, eyes, blood vessels and skeleton.

"People with severe cases, their eyes can literally pop out of their sockets and have to be popped back in," Isaacson said.

It appeared to doctors that Isaacson had a serious case of Marfan. The doctor said it was hard to narrow the exact severity of Isaacson's condition, but that it didn't look good. Isaacson asked for a timeline if his case was severe.

"Patients who have severe cases of it," the doctor said, "don't see thirty."

Isaacson asked for odds on longevity. "Maybe one in fifty, one in one hundred,'' the doctor said.

Isaacson kept the diagnosis a secret. He didn't want his remaining decade or so on Earth spent being constantly reminded of his condition. He was hell-bent on living life to the absolute fullest.

Isaacson didn't even inform his fiancée of the syndrome until seven months after the diagnosis. He told her that he would understand if she called off the marriage. But she went through with it and they were married in July 2000. Isaacson finally told family members of his condition in 2002, three years after being diagnosed.

Then something truly strange happened to Dan Isaacson's body. It behaved. It stayed relatively strong and clear of major side effects for five years after hearing that dreadful diagnosis inside the doctor's office. In late August 2005, Isaacson received another piece of life-changing news from his doctor.

"We should have seen problems by now," the physician said.

He went on to say that Isaacson wasn't out of the woods, but it was more likely than not that he had been spared the most serious form of Marfan. "Basically," the doctor said, "you will have the limitations you have now."

Isaacson pondered what to do with his life. It was the same question Frank Giannino had asked himself after setting the transcontinental world record twenty-five years earlier. Frank was twenty-eight years old trying to figure out how he could ever approach the thrill of running across America in world-record time. Giannino had felt the burden of reaching his mountaintop before age thirty.

Isaacson suddenly felt the unimaginable thrill that he would be able to celebrate his thirtieth birthday. He was twenty-five years old trying to decide what to do with his second chance at life.

"For the better part of five, six, seven years, all I was told was that I needed to take it easy," Isaacson said.

Shortly after the heavenly news, Isaacson took a two-week vacation to the island of Bora Bora, thirty-five miles northwest of Tahiti in the middle of the South Pacific. He was sitting in a restaurant when the idea hit him.

He would run across the United States.

"It was something to do because of the disease, to stop being told what my limitations were," he said. "I could do it over the summer."

Isaacson drew sponsorship from Nike, Champion and others. Bubba Gump Shrimp Company insisted on sponsoring the RV. In the summer of 2006, Isaacson began a 2,800-mile trek from Oregon to Illinois. His support team consisted of a friend driving the RV and a woman who had answered Isaacson's Craigslist ad requesting assistance. Isaacson had run marathons, but his training consisted largely of five-mile runs every other day.

Not surprisingly, by Day Four, Isaacson's tendons rubbed up against bones in both knees.

"An indescribable amount of pain," he said.

Isaacson flashed his modest ultra-running inexperience, just like Frank had in both his transcontinental runs. Isaacson didn't realize until three hundred miles into the run that he was placing undue wear on his legs by running solely against traffic. Runners must use both sides of the road to prevent problems caused by slanting road shoulders.

By Day Six, Isaacson was peeling entire sections of blisters from his feet. He had a few tricks up his sleeve as a former EMT, one of which involved the injection of baby Anbesol, the teeth-numbing solution, into affected blisters. Isaacson then used Super Glue – yes, Super Glue – to cover up openings created by the peeled blisters.

Isaacson suffered from bleeding lungs the entire run. He had only seventy percent lung capacity as a side effect of Marfan syndrome. Isaacson coughed up gobs of bright red blood at one point. The same thing had happened when he ran the Chicago

Marathon. He knew the symptoms – the taste of blood began permeating his throat. The culprit this time was the thinner air of elevation. Isaacson told his two-person support staff to expect the scene and not panic.

"Then all of a sudden, it started happening all day – day after day after day," Isaacson said. "I think Frank would probably agree. You have a very long conversation about yourself, about who you are and what you want to do."

Still, Isaacson had the cross-country runner's hardened interior that ignored the body's nasty proclamations. Somehow Isaacson managed to average thirty-five miles a day, just more than half of Frank's record-breaking daily allotment but a jaw-dropping achievement for a person with almost no ultra experience.

Isaacson was 708 miles from the finish when he found himself lost in Cicero, Illinois, once a hideout for Al Capone. Isaacson asked a guy for directions, but the man was far more interested in emptying Isaacson's wallet than helping the runner find his way.

"I'll take it all," the man said.

When Isaacson replied, "All of what?" the guy swiped a box cutter toward Isaacson's throat. Isaacson intercepted the blade with his left forearm, but the weapon stuck into Isaacson's flesh like an arrow plugging its target. All Isaacson remembered next was fighting the guy with a box cutter sticking from his forearm – three months of endorphins and frustrations colliding on a patch of Midwestern asphalt. What stands out most, though, was the noon-time crowd offering little more than a passing glance as they walked by.

Isaacson's transcontinental bid, needless to say, was over.

"This was more of a robbing of *me* than taking my wallet or any other stuff," Isaacson said. "It's been this unfinished business. To come so close to something and have it taken away from you. I can't promise I will beat the record. But I promise I can finish anything. Short of dying, I'm doing it."

The scene was set for *Chasing Frank*, a preliminary title to the documentary. But while Frank rejoiced in his life-changing run getting play on television, Klink delivered disheartening news. In researching the project, a Lucky Coffee Productions official spoke to an employee with Guinness Book of World Records.

The folks at Guinness apparently had decided to change the rules regarding Frank's milestone. Guinness had determined that the official record-breaking course must go from Los Angeles to New York, or vice versa. A Guinness official told Isaacson that the L.A.-New York route would be used because it is "more recognizable." Frank, of course, ran from San Francisco to New York.

Guinness further clouded its message by telling Isaacson that Frank's record would still stand. So his record-breaking run, in essence, would be recorded as going from L.A. to New York despite Frank running from San Francisco to New York.

The news was a jolt to the Lucky Coffee Productions people trying to prepare in case Isaacson broke the record. They needed to know the sanctioning standards for those trying to have a Guinness mark recognized. They most certainly needed to know if Frank would be credited as the record-holder.

"Once you are done, the (Guinness) committee reviews it and determines if it grants a record-breaking certificate," Isaacson said he learned from the company official. "I have to say, it was one of the weirder conversations I've ever had."

Guinness added yet another dose of confusion when contacted during the research for this book. "Frank Giannino's record is still current," wrote Sarah Wilcox, public relations and marketing executive for Guinness World Records North America, Inc. in an e-mail.

She attached the record-breaking passage used in Guinness' books and online material. Sure enough, it included the actual city from which Frank departed:

Fastest crossing of America (USA) on foot (male)
The fastest run across the USA is 46 days, 8 hr 36 min by Frank Giannino III (USA) for the 4,989 km (3,100 miles) from San Francisco to New York from 1 September 17 October 1980.

Guinness' mixed message perhaps best symbolized the triviality attached to one of the grittiest records in sports. The organization's decision to change the specified route while acknowledging Frank's record seemed to be the ultimate slap. Imagine Major League Baseball or the NFL or the NBA changing details of records because an aspect of the record might look better to a worldwide audience?

Given Guinness' plethora of oddball records, it was like the organization changing the listing that follows Frank's record on the Website page – fastest paddle board crossing of the Florida Straits (women's team) – to fastest paddle board crossing of Long Island Sound (women's team).

"To me, it completely symbolizes how people treat running in general," Isaacson said.

It was preposterous. It also lent evidence to the need for an accredited running organization, not Guinness, being the official source for transcontinental records. The folks behind Lucky Coffee Productions were determined to highlight the need for such a governing body.

"There should be a body that houses this information," Isaacson said, "that catalogs it."

Frank was disappointed by the strangely conflicting news. He couldn't understand why Guinness would favor the L.A.-New York route over the far more rigorous path from San Francisco that included tackling the Rocky Mountains. There was no comparison, Frank pointed out, in degree-of-difficulty in the courses.

"I'm not angry," he said. "I'm still figuring it out. I think that it's just a political reaction to a lot of influences. I think the majority of runners are in favor of the Los Angeles to New York route."

Frank sighed. "They can say what they want. All I know is what I did and how important it was to me and my family."

Isaacson believed Frank deserved a permanent place in the record book. Isaacson reasoned that even if someone were to break Frank's record, the runner would have benefited from the multitude of advancements since Frank's journey thirty-two years earlier. A bevy of fluid and other energy enhancements alone, such as electrolyte drinks and gels, have aided long-distance runners over the years. Running shoes today barely resemble those worn by Frank on his record-breaking run. Comparing Frank's record to any new holder was perhaps akin to rating latter-day home run records to those set in different eras amid deader baseballs and fewer hitter-friendly parks by guys without the benefit of strength-building substances and technology.

Perhaps most noteworthy, Frank's route is impossible to simulate entirely with some roads no longer existing.

"There is no possible way anybody can beat his record," Isaacson said.

Guinness not only opened Frank's eyes to the tenuous nature of his record. It reminded him of those casting doubt upon the legitimacy of his mark. Frank would never be able to combat such skepticism. Becky Wright, Frank's one-person crew during his first run across the country, still runs across doubters and naysayers.

"I would call my brothers and friends from the road and they would ask me, 'Is he really doing this? Is this a hoax?'" Becky said. "There were a lot of skeptics at the time. It was just so unbelievable that somebody could do something like that."

There remain many disbelievers all these years later. "Everyone says, 'Come on Becky, you can tell me,'" she said.

She tells them all the same thing. "He did every single mile that he said he did."

And that, Becky said, is "the great part – that he really, really did it. He did every single inch of it."

So you can imagine the level of doubt when Frank broke the record on his second run. It was one thing averaging 48.1 miles for sixty days covering 2,876 miles, as Frank did in 1979. It was, and is, the makings for a whole other sinkhole of skepticism when considering an average of 66.9 miles for forty-six days covering 3,103 miles, as he did on his record-breaking run a year later.

To take away the record would, in Frank's words, "insinuate that I'm a fraud" despite his documenting the run in detail, owning first-hand accounts from brother John, who biked alongside Frank, and possessing lengthy diary entries written by his step-mom Ja, remarried and living in Florida.

Frank said he started his run each morning precisely where he finished the previous day. "We always referred to a marker of some kind to mark the exact spot," he said. "I ran and walked every inch of the way. I was very meticulous about where the markers were."

He said that the distance he ran, if anything, was longer than his official measurement. "There were times that I missed a turn and had to back track," he said. Frank noted that he had run longer than his friend Marshall Ulrich, perhaps the top ultra-marathoner in history who had recently fallen short of breaking the record, "because I did not have GPS. I was not following the straightest line. For most of the run, I was on or paralleling U.S. Route 50, 40, then 30."

Frank even had something of an endorsement from Bruce Goldberg, the fourth crew member who left the team in Des Moines, Iowa, after butting heads with Frank's dad much of the way. Bruce had little interest in recounting the experience when contacted thirty-two years later. But he made one confirmation: Frank ran every step of the way under Goldberg's watch.

Frank no longer possessed all the paperwork submitted to Guinness. He said his copies were presented to Pyr Press, the local printing company that had assisted in helping publish Frank's ill-fated book following the run. Pyr owner Carol Boyle had no knowledge of such documentation when contacted for this book.

Frank realized that it was more important than ever for his story to reach the masses. He knew he would need the support of key individuals such as Ulrich if Guinness eventually decided to permanently erase the record.

And what if Guinness did decide to erase Frank's record from the books? He continually has insisted that he would have no problem with the record getting broken. But how would he cope with his greatest achievement, his claim to fame, treated as if it never happened?

How would anyone cope with that? Frank, as usual, took the high road.

"I'll just let it go," he claimed. "Nobody can ever accuse me of being a fraud with me knowing I ran every step of the way."

By now Frank had learned one cutting lesson since running across America: Skeptics are usually only a few steps behind. The complexities of monitoring and regulating such runs create an inviting path for doubters.

In fact, there is no disputing that the longest of long-distance runners occasionally have been known to spin long tales. Even Frank understands the inevitability of folks doubting the accuracy of a three thousand-mile record set by someone without a single sanctioned ultra race to his credit before running across the country in consecutive years.

Ulrich believes about two percent of runners, or more, exaggerate their accomplishments. He has heard whispers from those doubting Frank's run.

"People come to me and mention it," said Ulrich, well respected by the ultra community. "There have been a couple people that have kind of thrown it out there, not with anything whatsoever to back it up. My reply to them is, 'Listen, I can tell you he did it.' I know his character. He lives a life that is ethically and morally sound. That record seems to be pretty well bulletproof."

There was even an occasion when somebody else tried to claim Frank's record. John Wallace III, the organizer of usacrossers.com, was about to leave for his Los Angeles-to-New York run in October 2010. Or as Wallace put it in an e-mail, he was about "to break the thirty-year-old record of fastest crossing of the USA on foot" when he sent a note to former running great Rod Dixon, director of coaching and training for the LA Marathon. Copies went to Los Angeles-area runners, inviting folks to join him the first few days of the run.

That drew a response from Philip Steinman, L.A. Road Runners Pace Leader for the L.A. Marathon, noting that Reza Baluchi holds the record of seventy-seven miles a day, covering 3,300 miles in forty-three days from August-October 2009.

"Four people crewed Reza start to finish and documented his entire run," Steinman said. He went on to say that the effort was organized and produced by Keith Bowden's Castleland Productions, a Van Nuys, California, production company.

Perhaps Reza could go run the first ten miles with Wallace to wish him well," Steinman wrote in an e-mail. *Had he been invited and had a chance to know about John's ambitious plan in advance, I'm sure Reza would love to go say 'Hi', chat it up a bit over the first easy miles in Los Angeles and metaphorically pass the baton off to such a worthy candidate as John who might break Reza's record.*

That note, in turn, drew this response from Bowden, the CEO/Executive Producer of Castleland Productions, to Steinman and Dixon:

CORRECTION. The record needs to be clarified. Reza Baluchi does not hold the record for fastest run across America. Frank Giannino still holds the Guinness record for fastest run across America on foot in 1980 completing the run in 46 days, 8 hours and 36 minutes. Yes, it is true that I financed and produced Reza's attempt to beat that record, but it is a record that we cannot verify. I did have 4 people on the crew trying to document the run, but there were several cases in which Reza refused to have my team follow him and document him, including one period of time totaling almost 22 hours that we could not account for him. Which just so happens to be the day he covered the most miles. We have no proof that he actually ran the full journey across America. In fact, he refused to have my team document his arrival in New York City, so there is no one that is able to actually prove he ran the whole way or how he arrived in New York City.

"Just wanted to set the record straight. If a record attempt is to be made, it would be to beat Mr. Giannino's record from 1980. I wish you the best of luck in your run John. Godspeed and safe journey.

Wallace had impressive credentials, including a 3,804-mile run from Westport, Washington, to Tybee Island, Georgia, in

2004-05, in which he averaged 30.8 miles in 124 days. But on this occasion, Wallace's quest ended just short of ten days. He covered 421.2 miles.

Lucky Coffee's plan to follow Isaacson's quest for Frank's record morphed into discussions of a documentary, and perhaps a full-blown motion picture, solely about Frank's life. The entire plan eventually fizzled with the company apparently unable to sell the idea to prospective investors.

"The real issue was money," Frank said. "The money wasn't coming in. I think the other problem was people not believing it."

Fleeting fame was nothing new to Frank. He brushed aside the developments as he did any adversity. Frank long ago accepted that he wasn't going to become rich, and certainly not famous. He just wanted his story told.

23

Stan and Frank

The Guinness Book of World Records group wasn't the only body to leave a trail of ambiguity surrounding Frank's record. An influential segment of the ultra-running community passed on recognizing transcontinental records at all, no less Frank's mark. They remain skeptical of folks with little to no ultra experience churning out dozens and dozens of miles, day after day after day. And they have reserved their harshest criticism for the man whose record Frank broke: Stan Cottrell.

Cottrell was cited by Guinness as setting the world record when he averaged 64.55 miles daily from New York to San Francisco in early 1980. He broke Tom McGrath's record of 57.81 miles per day from New York to San Francisco three years earlier.

The ultra community frowned upon Cottrell's record almost immediately. Steve Clapp was editor of *Footnotes*, Road Runners Club of America's quarterly newspaper, in 1981 when he authored a two-part story that vilified Cottrell titled, "The Selling of Stan Cottrell." Clapp and others believed Cottrell was a fraud, and ripped several publications, including one of the nation's leading running magazines, *Runner's World*, for contributing "to the inflated reputation of ultra-marathoner Stan Cottrell."

Clapp reasoned that Cottrell had virtually no ultra background, and his high-profile pre-trans-con runs didn't "square with the facts." Clapp suggested that *Runner's World* had a stake in legitimizing Cottrell's record by earning "at least $70,000 in revenues from ads for products endorsed by him."

"Such hefty sums," Clapp wrote, "may help explain why running magazines scoffed at a subsequent claim by Frank Giannino, a sub-2:40 marathoner, to have broken Cottrell's record by running across the country in forty-six days wearing AAU brand shoes."

In an earlier *Footnotes* issue, Clapp cited Michael Chacour as proving a case against Cottrell's claim of a twenty-four-hour world record "since rejected by the National Running Data Center – and noted his bogus claims to have run the 1964 Boston Marathon in 2:52 (official time – 3:10:25) and to have qualified for the 1968 and 1972 Olympic marathon trials." Clapp noted that there was no qualifying standard for the '68 Olympic Trials marathon.

Nick Marshall, then an ultra-marathon authority for the National Running Data Center and an ultra-running historian, was among the loudest voices questioning Cottrell's credibility. Marshall condemned Cottrell's announced distance of 167.25 miles that set the twenty-four-hour world record, which according to *Running Times* magazine was twice listed as 167.5, a quarter-mile longer. The magazine reported Marshall telling Cottrell in a letter that the NRDC doesn't approve unmonitored solo efforts, and if it did, another runner, Andy West, would own the record after claiming a twenty-four-hour total of 167.488 miles in September 1978. The magazine reported that Rich Innamorato, a New York Road Runners Club official, pointed to Cottrell's distance appearing in print as 167.5 miles, besting West's total, after the correspondence between Marshall and Cottrell.

"Put bluntly," Marshall said in a letter to *Running Times*, "I'm the most knowledgeable person in the U.S. on ultra-marathoning in recent years, and I simply have yet to see any particularly credible evidence supporting Cottrell's claim.

"I have a natural tendency toward skepticism when a virtual unknown allegedly sets a world record in a solo exhibition. It's harder to run without competition, yet Cottrell supposedly ran his first hundred miles faster than any other American has ever done on the track ... and then proceeded to speed up after that, doing his fastest fifteen miles of the day from 112 to 127. If true, it doesn't just mean he's better than other American ultra-marathoners. It means this guy is in a class by himself. He's vastly superior to anyone I know of. I grant this is certainly possible. I just think it is unlikely."

Marshall went on to tear apart many claims by Cottrell, saying Cottrell never ran an organized ultra in his twenty-five years as a competitive runner, and that Cottrell failed to provide "verifiable dates, times and places" associated with his top performances.

A friend of Marshall's, Dan Brannen, also is an authority on ultra-running and dedicated to protecting the history of the sport through accurate documentation. Brannen was similarly critical of Cottrell when, in 2013, he was asked for comment. But wary of being hounded by Cottrell's lawyers, Brannen chose his words carefully.

"If you look at his history, his running history and other exploits," Brannen said, "he is not credible."

Brannen, executive director of the American Ultrarunning Association, chaired the USA Track & Field National Ultraruning Subcommittee for nine years. He also has a heady ultra-running background, like Marshall a nationally ranked competitor in the 1980s, and a former American record-holder for the forty-eight-hour run.

"I know what it's like," Brannen said of running well beyond the 26.2-mile marathon distance. "I know what it's like to see world-record holders struggle to run 10:00 per mile. I read day after day after day after day of him running seventy miles a day at 7:00 per mile. I don't even want to bother to explain how that's possible."

So if key members of the ultra community denounced or doubted Cottrell's claims, how did they view Frank Giannino and his record-breaking documentation? Brannen spent time with Frank shortly after his record-breaking run for an article Brannen was writing for *Running Times* on the history of transcontinental crossings.

Brannen organized and ran a two hundred-mile ultra-marathon race spanning the highest to lowest points of New Jersey, in fact beating some of the world's best ultra runners, Frank said, with a familiar method.

"He out-survived everyone," Frank said. "He was one of the remaining guys to finish."

Frank drove the course with Brannen beforehand and they got to know each other. "I did a little research on his background and found that he had reputable times," Brannen said. "When dealing with Frank, I felt that I was dealing with a guy that was credible. I rode in a car the length of New Jersey with him. I corresponded with him for a while. From the evidence I gathered about Frank, he's an honest, upstanding guy."

But Brannen stopped well short of rubber stamping Frank's record. "I have a personal policy," Brannen said. "You can't set a record for a solo performance. If you are asking me to verify Frank's record, I don't consider it a record.

"That's not impugning him," Brannen said. "The best anyone can call it is a 'claim.' I don't believe it's possible to produce documentation to, quote, 'prove' that anybody ran across the U.S. in a specific number of days unless it's run in a bona fide competition. I'm not calling for that. I think if you encourage it, if you create the impression that there are records for running across the U.S., eventually you are going to get people claiming them, and they are going to be suspect."

He continued, "I don't mean to suggest that doing what he did that Frank's been the cause of that. I just don't believe in supporting that type of pursuit. I am not going to ignore them, because some of them were done by individuals who have very long and strong records of being top performers. There's value to it. I ignore ... not only ignore, but am opposed to, the keeping of records" from runs outside of bona fide competitions. There are all sorts of claims out there."

He said he believed that if the general public viewed such runs as legitimate venues for record-setting, it tended to diminish accomplishments in more officially sanctioned competitions. To that end, Brannen has had a major problem with the *Guinness Book of World Records* for highlighting, and in essence legitimizing, trans-con records. "I think the *Guinness Book of World Records* does the sport of ultra-marathoning a disservice," Brannen said.

As for Frank, when asked how he was viewed in the ultra community, Brannen said flatly, "He's not."

Brannen said current members of the ultra community don't pay attention to trans-con runs or trans-con runners. "If you asked them who Stan Cottrell and Frank Giannino are," Brannen said, "99.5 percent wouldn't know them. It's not on the current ultra community's radar."

In 2013, Cottrell said Marshall and others have "ruined my life," tarnishing his reputation to the point of chasing away prospective sponsors and killing his income sources. Claiming he once earned $70,000-$100,000 annually off running, Cottrell said he was getting by on $1,100 monthly Social Security payments, and that he has had numerous speaking engagements denied or canceled because of bad publicity.

"In the past three years," Cottrell said in his Southern twang, "I haven't made one penny. They made up one lie after another after another. It's just sick. Nick Marshall considers himself the ultra-marathoning running expert in the world. I guess this fella or this group feels like they are going to be the great purveyors of truth, and it's all ridiculous."

Cottrell, who said he's never met Marshall, said the accusations began shortly after his record-setting run across America, and that he was talked out of suing Marshall at the time by Fred Lebow, the late founder of the New York City Marathon. Cottrell said Lebow felt the suit would "hurt running and set running back in a major way."

Tyler Dixon, Cottrell's lawyer, said in an e-mail that he's aware of the negative articles written back in the '80s:

A small minority of people (none of whom ever ran with Stan or even saw him run) rejected Stan's 24-hour run and his cross-USA run. I offered to show his detractors the signed lap sheets for the twenty-four-hour run, but they declined. Stan invited them to run with him, but they declined. After the 1980 trans-USA run, they were shown his daily logs (again with each daily

entry being signed by those present during that day), and they
complained that they were too neat and did not describe enough
'bad days.' Stan is a positive person, and rarely expresses
negativity, so for him to write during a day that he had troubles
with blisters, or that he lost his big toe nail, etc., would be
contrary to his character and personality. He often lost toenails,
and got blisters and cramps, and encountered other difficulties
that were often a problem – but Stan's view was to simply write
the distance covered and what he saw – and in his eyes he saw
beauty, the beauty of this vast country. He looks to the positive.

Stan's epic runs have done more for good will, friendship,
health and fitness than all the ultra-distance competitive races
combined, but a small group of self-appointed elitists, who claim
to be the only authority that counts, denigrate such events. They
feel that if it is not a race, it is a 'farce.' That is the word Nick
Marshall has used to describe long point-to-point runs like those
of Stan and Frank.

Nick Marshall started the 'controversy' (which we deem a
fabrication), and takes pride in that fact – but refused to run with
Stan, and admits he has never seen Stan run. This small group
raised their heads again in 1985 when Stan and some Chinese
runners ran across the country relay-style. My older son was on
the trip and can attest to the accuracy of the running claims.

Stan went on to do many runs throughout the world, and
those negative articles had no impact whatsoever, according to
his lawyer:

I can say this. In 1981, I reviewed the signed lap sheets and
interviewed most of the lap counters on the 24-hour run, who
confirmed the accuracy of their count. The run was well
publicized in advance, so many people were there to witness the
run. No one doubted the veracity of the mileage or times.

But Nick Marshall took it upon himself to claim it was a fraud
simply because he had never heard of Stan – even though
Running Times published an article in March 1979 referencing a
multi-day run through Georgia Stan had done to raise money for
a charity, mentioning that it was a training run in preparation

for Stan's upcoming attempt to break the 24-hour run record. In '81 or '82, I also interviewed two of the four trans-USA crew members (on the 1980 run across America) who confirmed he had traversed the entire distance on foot. I could not locate the other two, and know that one claims (even though he was in the advance team and seldom saw Stan run) that there were questions raised by another crew member about whether Stan was running the entire distance.

It just so happens that that 'other' crew member was one of those I interviewed back in the early '80s who confirmed that while he was on the run, Stan ran the entire distance. Since then I have interviewed another person who was on that run 35 to 38 of the 48 days, and he confirms that he personally observed Stan run the entire distance. He also confirmed that he frequently observed the crew filling out and signing the daily log, and that for the days he read the log, it was accurate. In my opinion, there can be no honest doubt about Stan having completed these runs as claimed.

Cottrell said he had enough with Marshall and a handful of other harsh critics. But Cottrell's side didn't name Marshall in a lawsuit dated July 2011. The suit instead named five people who allegedly had a hand in smearing Cottrell's name with a series of Internet accusations, including characterizing Cottrell as a "scam artist" involved in all sorts of deception.

Cottrell said he had more than ninety witnesses and five thousand pages of documents proving the accuracy of his claims. Said Dixon via e-mail:

The suit seeks damages, but all Stan has really wanted was for the defamatory posts to be taken down with an agreement that the defendants would not post any future negative statements about Stan. In short, Stan and his family just want these people to leave them alone so they can have their lives back. We made that offer several times and they rejected it. Stan had two contracts, and had funding for his global friendship run, but when the defendants' defamatory blog and other actions started, the supporters backed away. Stan lost considerable revenue, and that is one of the elements of damage included in the suit.

In these days of the Internet, the defendants have managed to promote their agenda, giving these early naysayers a greater audience than they ever had before. So Stan is having to prove all over again that he is what he says he is, and that he has done what he says he has done.

In March 2014, the jury came back with a judgment in favor of Cottrell to the tune of $635,000.
Said Dixon an another e-mail:

The vast majority of those who run believe that adventure runs are as important as or even more important than races. In fact, there is an article in the Wall Street Journal *on that very point. The late Fred Lebow, long time President of the NY Road Runners Club, welcomed the advent of the adventure run, and pointed out as early as 1979 that adventure running would be at the heart of a running boom. He was correct. I wish he were alive today to testify. He is the one who talked Stan out of suing Nick Marshall back in 1985 or '86 -- saying that Marshall and his cronies were a small minority, and that few people paid attention to them – and that in time, it would all die down. He told Stan a suit at that time would be bad for running. Stan heeded Fred's advice, and for decades it appeared that Fred was correct. Nothing further was heard from Nick and friends while Stan went about his international runs promoting international good will. Heads of state have complimented and encouraged the type of 'sports diplomacy' carried out by Stan. But there will always be those who denigrate such laudable things. People who are not guided by good will do not understand events that are intended to promote good will – because they don't care about good will. It's been 33 years since the 1979 24-hour run that Nick objected to and he is still not over it, and begrudges the notoriety Stan has received for doing runs to promote good will and friendship (while raising money for charities). Truly amazing what some people will resent.*

Ironically, Cottrell admitted that he once raised a couple eyebrows toward the runner who erased his mark from the record book: Frank Giannino. Cottrell, remember, paid Frank a surprise visit in Illinois to check up on Frank, and that according to Cottrell – and separately confirmed by Frank – they ran seventy miles together. Cottrell left the next morning after spending the night with Frank inside his motor home.

"He had it all worked out, how much he needed to average a day to break my record," Cottrell said.

Cottrell said his skepticism was drawn from witnessing a deep gash in Frank's foot. Cottrell believed there was no way Frank could run the final thousand miles or so, including the rugged Pennsylvania terrain, in record-breaking time given the injury. For his part, Frank said the cut wasn't all that deep.

"I'm going to tell you the truth because that's the only thing I know," Cottrell said. "I remember his foot was frayed open on the bottom. There was a gash, like a deep cut, on the forefoot. His foot looked like hamburger meat. I've never, ever seen a cut like he had. It looked like his foot needed to be sutured. I remember looking at the foot and just thinking, 'How in the world can he walk on that foot, let alone run on it.' Pennsylvania is a tough stretch to run across – lots of ups and downs, ups and downs, ups and downs. One day I did everything I possibly could do (in Pennsylvania) and it was thirty-four miles."

Said Frank, "I had heavy calluses and they broke open on the right foot more," Frank said. As for Stan's description of the foot resembling hamburger meat, Frank thinks Stan exaggerated the injury.

Were sutures required?

"No," Frank said.

Cottrell quickly added, "And this is not a putdown. This is not me taking any issue with Frank's performance or anything whatsoever. I think Frank is an honorable man. His parents were wonderful people. They had water for me, drinks for me."

Cottrell said he has heard criticism directed at Frank in the ultra community. Three decades after their runs, Cottrell views Frank fondly.

"We were two fellas that … let's say at that particular time, Frank and I were bona fide nuts in the eyes of the world," Cottrell said. "We didn't think we were nuts. It was about human performance. It was about accepting a challenge and dealing with it. Every day was a new challenge. We were pioneers."

Regarding his seventy-mile run with Frank, Cottrell said, "There was a bond there that we have that has picked up to where we are on Mile Seventy-one."

Cottrell, now seventy-three, said he spent part of the Fall of 2013 getting depositions from folks to support his defamation case. He asked Frank if he would sign a deposition backing Cottrell, given their seventy-miler in Illinois. Frank agreed to vouch for Cottrell regarding their run together. Frank had no evidence that would confirm or denounce Cottrell's claims before or after their day together on the roads. But Frank, who has made a living fitting orthotics and is well-schooled in the technical elements of the sport, had no problem speaking favorably of Cottrell's ability to run long distances.

"He was very fluid, a natural runner," Frank said. "He had no biomechanical issues at all. He could run. I watched his gait. I have no doubt about his abilities."

Frank was driving back from Boston in early October 2013 when he spoke to Cottrell for the first time in three decades. Cottrell talked excitedly about a couple of adventure runs he wanted to do, including run seventy miles – to mark his age – in every country. He also floated an idea of joining Giannino and a handful of other masters runners who had successfully completed trans-con runs, and doing a relay across America for charity.

"I do a lot with orphans all over the world," Cottrell said. "It would be a fun time and the press could get the word out. Frank is a legend. We ultimately made our mark. It would be a statement to the world that you are never too old to dream big."

Frank politely declined, citing his hectic work schedule and leg issues preventing him from churning out much more than three-mile runs.

"I know there have been statements made about some of his claims from the past," Frank said. "I cannot validate whether they are true or not. All I know is that Stan ran seventy miles with me years ago and the experience was a positive one. His ability to cover great distances, to me, is real and I believed he successfully ran across America as he claimed."

His chat with Cottrell concluded an exciting day for Frank. He had gone to Boston to meet up with an old friend, Dave McGillivray, to discuss aspects of this book. McGillivray ran across the country in 1978, immediately preceding Frank's first trans-con run. McGillivray ran 3,452 miles from Medford, Oregon, to his hometown of Medford, Massachusetts, in eighty days, averaging 43.7 miles daily, before finishing in Fenway Park. He celebrated his twenty-fourth birthday during the run.

"I think I was the youngest," McGillivray said. "And I think I ran farther than anyone. But with me, it wasn't about going for a record or anything."

McGillivray's quest, as chronicled in his book, *The Last Pick*, was to show the limitless potential of an undersized athlete who, as a kid, was often chosen last for teams. In 1981, he created Dave McGillivray Sports Enterprises (DMSE), a firm that manages road race events, and in 1988, he was named race director of perhaps the most successful and best known 26.2-milers in the world, the Boston Marathon.

"When I(ran across the country, it was a big deal," McGillivray said inside his office at the Boston Athletic Association. "I was on *Good Morning America.*"

All these years later, McGillivray can relate to negativity surrounding successful endeavors in general and Frank and Stan's runs in particular. "The worst part of success," he said, quoting Bette Midler, "is finding someone who is happy for you."

McGillivray has a thick file filled with thoughts and ideas on an organized and sanctioned race across America. He is open to the idea but too consumed with race directing chores to organize all aspects of a trans-con. McGillivray, though, allowed that he would gladly take a lesser role in putting together the event if the proper organization was in place. In fact, McGillivray – who upon turning twelve years old, started marking each birthday by running the mileage equivalent of his age (now sixty) – is even interested in being one of the runners.

Perhaps no one would be happier to see it all come to fruition in the form of a reality series than Frank Giannino.

"There's my dream," Frank said. "Engage the global running community. Have each runner GPS-ed so you know where they are at all times."

It certainly would be a long way from maps and TripTiks and one-person support staffs.

24

Why? The Answer

Frank is like many people who, as they grow older, wonder about their impact on others. He wasn't a teacher or a high school coach or the like, professions in which his influence could be easier to quantify.

Frank has inspired many folks, to be sure. But his greatest collective contribution will be to the people he resembles most: the person next door walking into his running-themed shoe store for help.

They reveal their doubts and fears and inhibitions as well as their hopes and goals, emotions with which Frank is quite familiar. Some of them walk in unsure of exactly what they are searching for, knowing only that they need comfort and, perhaps, clarity. Frank can't help them all. Even the best orthotics can't cure certain foot issues or deeper-rooted pain. But Frank sees a little of himself in all of them, mostly a guy trying to make a living and do the right thing beneath the potentially paralyzing distractions and negativity of life.

"I'm in a place of peace and confidence like I've never been before in my life," he said. "I'm not really trying to inspire the masses as I am trying to inspire one person at a time. Some people need the praise of millions. I need the recognition that I'm doing something useful one person at a time.

"Nothing gives me the satisfaction of seeing a person in pain and I'm able to do something to help them. Your physical health is a reflection of the rest of your life. I am constantly trying to help people believe that they can do it, too. I latched onto it because I knew I could, and the fact that other people found it exceptional provided me with all the inspiration I needed."

Amid those torturous days trying to keep his business afloat, when bill collectors called as his inventory shrunk, Frank rediscovered his purest calling – road race management; specifically, helping to revive his hometown race, the Orange Classic 10K in Middletown.

Once perennially ranked among *Runner's World* magazine's top road races in the U.S. with world-class fields and two thousand runners strong, the Orange Classic had disbanded following the twenty-fifth running in 2005. Major sponsors had bowed out.

Frank and buddy Bob Bright, who passed away in 2009 at age fifty-seven, had designed the race's original course, and Frank was the Orange Classic's first director. He couldn't let the event die. So he teamed with two other local running enthusiasts, Wayne Beam and George Shurter, to get the ball rolling. The new Orange Classic – now called The Classic – made its debut in 2006.

Frank and his fellow race directors weren't trying to save a Middletown road race as much as they were trying to save the community spirit that sprouts from Middletown to Montreal, from Kingston to Kenya, folks from the neighborhood and from the world sharing a bond in small-town America each June.

Frank knew the race had to continue. He knew that you can't start canceling tradition. First a road race. Then a county fair. Next thing you know, the folks gathering for youth soccer games are joyless strangers united by nothing more than the chosen sport of their young.

"We are going to see Frank twenty years from now, and he is still going to be putting shoes on feet," said Beam, who has known Frank for four decades. "He's going to be doing what he loves to do. You can look at Frank and see he's never going to be rich, never going to be a movie star. He had that – and he still has it – that 'no-quit' in him. He will bug you to death until he gets his way. Even today, he's sixty-four years old and still has more energy than anybody I know. The guy doesn't stop."

The Classic officials added a 5K and kept the world-class influence of Kenyan runners mixed with standout Americans. Frank Shorter, who grew up in Middletown and trained on parts of The Classic course, appears at the race annually. The Classic has drawn steady twelve hundred-runner fields, not quite as large as its heyday, but time changes everything and everybody. Sometimes smaller is better, whether it's a road race or a business or a man's eternal search for prosperity and happiness.

Frank moved his store, Frank's Custom Shoe-Fitting, yet again in July 2015, to a more favorable location less than a mile away on the same side of the same road in Middletown. In April 2016, he estimated the business would produce its best annual numbers ever, up to $600,000, with a long-term goal of $750,000 and an ultimate goal of $1 million. With Frank, life is still about setting and reaching goals, but also, more than ever, it's about experiencing pure happiness.

"I've always believed in myself," he said, tapping his chest. "I think I can out-survive anything."

He and wife Michele have a planned vacation for this summer – the summer of 2016 – hopping among three islands in Hawaii. Michele is retiring in June after thirty-two years of teaching. Michele and Frank are about to fulfill their dream of traveling like they did early in their marriage.

"I'm okay with me," Frank Giannino said. "I think everyone lives in fear that their life didn't matter. A big hole in my heart closed up when I got involved in The Classic. One of the life lessons I learned was that you are not going to have everyone like you, and that's okay. It's an ongoing process. There's a fine line of, 'When is it okay for you not to care about other people in how they act or feel toward you?' I still wear my heart on my sleeve helping people."

Frank's runner's high was revived by his zeal for community events and the camaraderie they produce. The Classic reminded him of one of the reasons he twice ran across the United States of America. It helped provide the most basic answer to that gnawing question: "Why run across the country?"

The answer for Frank is that there is no sport, no activity – perhaps nothing else in life, still – that brings him such pleasure and fulfillment.

The only tangible remnants from his record-breaking run are a jacket reading, "AAU Shoes Run Coast to Coast." Frank is unsure what came of his finish-line hat and shirt. Most of the snapshots from the run are gone, but he savors those in his collection.

He went through a rocky marriage ending in divorce. He fought through harsh financial woes and businesses teetering toward bankruptcy. But Frank still had the world record for the fastest run across America. He still had a wife and a family providing unconditional love.

And he still had the passion that he took to the roads 3½ decades earlier.

Now returning to his roots as a race director, he realized more than ever that he had an unbreakable bond with running, that even as a light recreational jogger, Frank Giannino is still running for his life.

"Running has saved my life, my entire life," he said. "It was the one thing that has made me feel good. I can't tell you the unbelievable feeling of breaking from the pack. Oh my God, I think it's one of the greatest feelings on Earth.

"In the end, life is a series of short stories, each with its own unfolding. I found my place in running early on. You put your shoes on and go until you can't go anymore."

Epilogue

Marijean Giannino, oldest sister
May 10, 1946-October 23, 2006

Frank Giannino Jr., father
April 1, 1922-December 2, 2000

Ruth Hitchens-Giannino, mother
April 7, 1925-March 19, 1974

Just before the release of the book, I asked Frank to sum up his prevailing feelings about his parents. His answer provided not only a critical look at their relationships, but it unveiled yet another layer of Frank himself. Despite hundreds of hours interviewing Frank and his insistence on transparency, he didn't reveal until the week of the book's deadline that he has suffered bouts of depression. The outwardly ebullient man with a gift for gab had endured inner struggles even deeper than he had admitted.

In fact, Frank's failure to mention the 'D' word earlier is symmetrical to his mind set while twice running across the United States. He was able to complete the runs – finishing the second run in record-breaking fashion – by not only blocking out negatives such as pain and support-team distractions, but by dismissing them altogether.

The passing of Frank's three oldest immediate family members has brought him varied emotions over the years. All three had a profound effect on him, not always positive. Frank and his dad had a deep bond. Frank considers his mom the source of his self-esteem issues that haunted him all the way into adulthood.

A few years ago, with Frank on the other side of sixty years old and Ruth buried in the Walden, New York, cemetery near where he grew up, Frank searched for words to sum up his biological mother.

"It's been a long time since I visited her grave," he said one day.

In fact, Frank had forgotten which day his mom had died and the location of her plot. He wasn't sure why he had stayed away, but he felt bad about it. When that was brought up, Frank almost immediately paid his mom a visit. He felt better afterward and soon planned to return with his family.

"Not visiting was never about not caring," Frank said.

Frank and his sister Marijean eventually became tight, but his closeness to Dad brought frustration from his mother and a special resentment from Marijean.

She was devastated when Frank was born, seeing him as one more obstacle in the strained relationship with her father. Marijean didn't feel she received the same affection from Dad as Frank did, and she could never understand why Frank put his dad on a pedestal. But she became Frank's biggest supporter through adulthood. She was always there for him, and Frank adored her.

As Frank puts it, "In death comes clarity."

In many cases, in death also comes forgiveness. His words recently:

"My mother and father were the biggest influences of my life. I didn't view them as close to one another. There was a distance between them. But they were both very dedicated to their marriage and to their five children. They were also very close to their own siblings. I fondly remember the many trips we took to Auburn, New York, to visit with grandparents, cousins and lots of relatives.

"In sharing my story, many emotions have surfaced about growing up with Mom and Dad. I believe that in death comes clarity. I do feel that my mom battled depression, and so did my father. I have battled with it myself. Whatever events took place, and there were many, I can look back at my time with Mom and Dad as among the most cherished times of my life. If it weren't for them and the decisions they made as parents, both good and not so good, I do not believe I would have made the choices I did later in life, both good and not so good.

"I have few regrets about my parents. I do know this. I'm as optimistic as ever. I love my family. I have great friends. I look forward to every day and what it brings, and I can thank my parents, both perfect and imperfect, for who I am today. Thank you, Mom and Dad, for everything!"

Josephine Giacalone
The Unsung Hero

Josephine Giacalone was a schoolmate of both Frank's father and mother, and the Giacalones and Gianninos were family friends through the years. She appeared well on her way to a life of being single when she attended Ruth's wake and got to talking with Frank's dad. They quickly realized how much they had in common and, only six months after Ruth's passing, Josephine and Frank Jr. were married.

"Ja can adapt to any atmosphere," Frank III said of his step-mom. "She was one hundred percent loyal to Dad. I saw them debate and discuss, but I never saw them argue, not once."

Ja also was a spectacular cook, a quality that pulled her step-son to the finish line every bit as powerfully as the work of Sonny or John.

"After it was all over with, I was real tired," Ja said years later. "I had no ambition to do anything. I just rested. It took a while to get my energy back."

As for her contributions? "Oh, I don't want to toot my own horn," she said. "I managed to compromise and do things. There were a lot of things I wanted to see along the way, but we didn't have time for it."

Ja and Sonny moved to Ocala, Florida, in 1988 after her doctor suggested she live in a kinder climate after a bad bout of pneumonia. Three years after Sonny passed away, Ja was back in her hometown of Auburn, New York, attending a church bazaar when she ran into Carmen Salva.

They had met fifty-one years earlier when Carmen asked Ja to dance at a restaurant in Auburn. They danced again a week later at the restaurant but never got together. He would spend time in the Navy, get married and have five children. His wife, like Ja's husband, passed away in 2000.

Carmen and Ja were married in 2004 and live in Ocala, Florida. Ja is ninety years old and has maintained her health despite having an aortic valve replaced in 2001 and periodically battling vertigo.

Becky Wright
The One-Person Support Team

Becky Wright was a twenty-three-year-old substitute teacher assisting the girls' track coach at a local high school when she met Frank at his friend's running shoe store in New Paltz, New York. She knew of Frank's long distance running through her brother, Mike, who had run with Frank years earlier at Valley Central High School. Becky had taken up running herself and, with a sense of adventure and an open mind, she agreed to become Frank's support driver for his first run across the United States.

Seeing firsthand the endurance and stamina Frank displayed inspired Becky to become more courageous in her own life's pursuits. She rock-climbed, backpacked, kayaked and owned horses for many years. She reached her goal to teach and enjoyed a fulfilling twenty-year career before retiring three years ago.

Becky, now fifty-nine, met her husband shortly after the run. They have two children. She has taken up pottery and has a small studio at her home. She credits Frank's strength and fortitude with helping her overcome some of her own life's obstacles such as a hip replacement and malignant melanoma. "Seeing the physical pain Frank endured gave me the strength to push through some of my more painful experiences," she said during a recent visit.

As for Frank's unfulfilled feelings after finishing the run, Becky said, "To me, he achieved his goal. I watched him run across the country. He did it."

Frank is the first to say that he couldn't have done it without Becky. There would have been no second run; no record-setting performance or place in the *Guinness Book of World Records*. When that notion is brought to light, Becky smiles. They made each other better, not for two months, but for a lifetime.

John Giannino
The Iron Man

If there ever was a perfect crew member, it was John Giannino, Frank's brother. John was seventeen years old and entering his senior year of high school when he rode a bicycle alongside Frank during his record-breaking run. John had the perfect even temperament, and he was unconditionally dedicated to helping his brother. He had no bike training or special riding experience, and he often had to push the bike up hills. He was sometimes so fatigued that he slept on the shoulder of roads.

But John's complaints were minimal. As part of a crew including their dad, Frank Jr., step-mom Ja and publicity man Bruce Goldberg, John became known as the Iron Man for his mental and physical toughness.

Thirty-six years later, he hasn't changed a bit.

John Giannino has worked in the same correctional facility for thirty years now, handling the graveyard shift the past sixteen years. John was eligible for retirement five years ago, but he's not ready for that just yet.

In July, he will celebrate with wife Lisa his twenty-fifth wedding anniversary. They have two children: Sean, a freshman running hurdles for his high school track team; and Alannah, twenty, fresh off her own painful journey.

She has a temperament similar to her dad's, which certainly has come in handy lately. Alannah was brushing her teeth one day in June 2015 when she noticed something resembling a cluster of grapes hanging from the inside of her throat.

"Dad," she called to John, "can you come look at something?"

It was a rare childhood cancer that typically victimizes two- to three-year-olds. The prognosis was good, John said, and in January 2016 Alannah completed six months of treatments.

"She's like me, like, 'So what?'" John said. "She was right on top of it when she was first diagnosed. She did all the research herself."

This fall Alannah will return to college at SUNY New Paltz, one of Uncle Frank's college stomping grounds.

John received his own education biking alongside his brother across America. He caught up on his work after returning to school and wound up earning a New York State Regents diploma. Like Frank, John attended the local two-year college, Orange County Community College in Middletown. He had visions of becoming an aeronautical engineer but realized that his math background was too limited to pursue the field. John landed a job in corrections, like his dad. But unlike his dad, a male nurse, John became a corrections officer.

Since 1998, he's lived in a quiet neighborhood in a town called Pine Bush, eight miles from his hometown of Walden.

John has done most of the work on his home, including plumbing, electrical and sheetrock. People ask how he learned to do it all and John's answer is simple.

"My dad."

He remains close to Frank despite their eleven-year age difference. They still reminisce about the time they crossed America together.

"I can't begin to tell you how much pleasure it gives me to be around John," Frank said. "I've never had an argument with my brother over anything."

"His memory is a lot more vivid of it than mine," John said of the run. "I don't know how many times I watched my father cut away at his feet, cut the dead tissue. It's astounding to me that (Frank's record) has lasted this long. There have been a lot of people with better finances; a lot have been better runners than him – and they have failed."

There was no such failure in the Fall of 1980, when a teenager pedaled most of Frank's 3,103-mile route to earn his nickname, the Iron Man.

Pat Perry
The Joiner

Frank and Pat Perry kept in touch for about a decade after meeting by chance near Pat's Ohio home during the record-breaking run. Pat had gone into a gym to work out, but instead saw Frank's parked motor home and watched from a window inside the gym. He finally came out to greet Frank, and by day's end, Frank had set a one-day personal record by clocking 73.4 miles.

Pat Perry, who had never gone beyond the 26.2-mile marathon wall, had run forty-three of those miles with Frank.

A month later, Pat ran his first ultra race, a fifty-miler in Toledo, Ohio. He ran two more ultras, including – two years after meeting Frank – the prestigious Western States 100-Mile Endurance Run in California. He saw a story in *Sports Illustrated* about the Hawaii Ironman, the ultimate triathlon test consisting of a 2.4-mile swim, 112-mile bike and 26.2-mile run. Perry completed it in 1982, then did it again in '83.

At last count he's done those two Ironmans, eighteen marathons and four ultras.

"If I hadn't run with Frank," Perry said, "none of that would have happened."

They got together days after Frank's run when he returned the motor home to Ohio and met with his sponsor. Then they lost touch. Frank longed to re-open the gift of their friendship. Internet search upon search, phone listing upon listing, failed to locate Pat Perry from Youngstown, Ohio.

Then one day in Spring 2014, Frank answered the phone at his store. The caller asked if Frank Giannino came to the store often, that it was Pat Perry from Youngstown, Ohio. Pat was between jobs and feeling a bit melancholy. He had checked out an ultra running video on YouTube when he came across another video. It was Frank's promotional footage for his new store, with a phone number attached.

"Frank is one of those people who, if you don't talk to him in a million years, when finally do, you feel like you talked to him an hour ago," Pat said.

There would be no more communication gaps, no more forks in the road between pupil and teacher, teacher and pupil.

Pat, the manager of an Athlete's Foot store when he met Frank, endured a devastating divorce that made him question his inner being and left him searching for his purpose in life. He eventually wrestled out of his doldrums and continues a remarkable ascension in the shoe apparel business, most recently helping develop the 361 Degrees shoe line in the United States The company is a sponsor of the coming Summer Olympics in Rio. Pat's goal is for 361 Degrees to be among the top five footwear/apparel brands in the world by 2025.

"I'm working my ass off and I've been really, really lucky," he said recently. "It's been an incredible ride. The long and the short of it is, we keep making good products and we keep making better products.

"Frank and I have been lucky enough to make a career out of an addiction. What Frank did for me, I've tried to do for others."

What Frank did for Pat was teach him the power of perseverance, that virtually no amount of pain or suffering can keep a healthy mind from reaching goals.

Perry talked about reaching that point in ultras and Ironmans when your body is done, depleted, finished, but your mind remains sharp and tells you, "Bullshit, come on. All the sacrifices you made and all the sacrifices family and friends made, you selfish bastard, and now you are going to quit because you are tired? Then there comes the point when you are mentally shot and your body says to your brain, 'Jerkwad, you told me to do this. You get back in the game.'

"Somewhere down the road, your mind and body agree that you are done. At that point, you go to a place that you didn't even know you had, and you keep going.

"That was a place I didn't even know existed as I was staring at Frank. I had no frame of reference. But what I wanted, he had. I didn't know what that was, but he had it and I wanted it."

Pat Perry eventually found that place, in competition, in life, a journey that began one day in front of a gym in Boardman, Ohio.

Frank's Route for his Record-Breaking Run
Sept. 1-Oct. 18, 1980

All measurements are a combination of Frank's brother John Giannino's bicycle odometer and/or mileage readings from the motor home. Today, of course, we use Global Positioning System (GPS) to reveal direction and measure distances. GPS is typically the method used by modern-day journey runners.

Sept. 1: 55 miles
San Francisco, California, City Hall steps
- Polk Street to left on Bay Street
- Right on Laguna
- Left on Marina Boulevard which becomes Mason Street
- To Lincoln Boulevard
- To vista access and onto the northbound walkway of Golden Gate Bridge
- Across the bridge to Conzelman Road
- Right onto East Road
- To Alexander Avenue
- To South Street
- To Second Street
- To Bridgeway Boulevard, Sausalito
- Onto bike trail
- To Scott Valley, exit bike trail
- On and off bike trails and residential streets to Route 37, south of Novato
- On Route 37 (also known as Sears Point Road), cross the Richard Janson Bridge
- Left onto Flosden Road
- Right onto American Canyon Road
- Day ends at I-80 and American Canyon Road

Sept. 2: 50 miles
- Day begins at American Canyon Road and I-80
- Then onto McGarey Road paralleling I-80
- Left on Red Top Road
- Right on Jameson Canyon Road
- To West Cordelia Drive
- Left on Lopes Road
- To right on Business Center Drive which become Suisun Parkway
- Onto Abernathy Road
- Onto Auto Mall Parkway
- Left on West Texas Street
- Right on Oliver Road
- To right on Travis
- Onto Holiday Lane

- To right on Barbour Drive
- To Waterman Road
- To Martin Road
- To Hilborn Road
- To Lyon Road
- To right on Cherry Glenn Road
- Left on Rivera Road
- To Cherry Glen Road
- Across to Butcher Road
- Left on Alamo
- Right on Merchant
- Right on Mason
- Left on Depot
- Right on W. Monte Vista Avenue
- To East Monte Vista Avenue
- To right on Nut Tree Road
- To left on Orange Drive
- Left on Leisure Town Road
- Right onto Quinn Road
- To Oday Road
- To Milk Farm Road
- To Sparling Lane
- To Olmo Lane
- To Old Davis Road in Davis, California
- To Second Street
- To County Road 32A
- To West Capitol Avenue
- To Tower Bridge Gateway and the day's finish at the Sacramento River

Sept. 3: 50 miles
- Tower Bridge in Sacramento, California
- Onto to the Capitol Mall
- To right on 9th Street
- Left on N Street
- To Capitol Avenue
- To Folsom Boulevard
- To Iron Point Road in Folsom, California
- To U.S. 50
- To Tong Road which becomes Country Club Drive
- Onto U.S. 50
- To Placerville where day ends at the beginning of the Expressway. Police won't let us enter the Expressway during rush-hour traffic, so we wait until morning to get on U.S. 50 well before the sun comes up.

Sept. 4: 53 miles
- Begin on the Expressway U.S. 50 in Placerville, California
- Stay on U.S. 50 all day

- Finish just shy of Echo Summit near South Lake Tahoe

Sept. 5: 50 miles
- Begin on U.S. 50 just shy of Echo Summit
- Continue on U.S. 50 through South Lake Tahoe, California to Carson City, Nevada
- Merge with U.S. 395 in Stewart, Nevada
- U.S. 50 and South Carson Street are the same
- Stay on South Carson Street
- Turn right on East William Street aka U.S. 50E
- 10 miles on U.S. 50

Sept. 6: 63 miles
- 10 miles east of Carson City on U.S. 50
- To 11 miles east of Fallon on U.S. 50
- Entire day spent on U.S. 50
-

Sept. 7: 60 miles
- 11 miles east of Fallon on U.S. 50
- To 37 miles west of Austin, Nevada on U.S. 50

Sept. 8: 46 miles
- 37 miles west of Austin on U.S. 50
- To 9 miles east of Austin on U.S. 50

Sept. 9: 60 miles
- 9 miles east of Austin on U.S. 50
- To 9.5 miles east of Eureka , Nevada on U.S. 50

Sept. 10: 60 miles
- 9.5 miles east of Eureka on U.S. 50
- To 5 miles west of Ely, Nevada on U.S. 50

Sept. 11: 70.8 miles
- 5 miles west of Ely on U.S. 50
- 5 miles east of Nevada-Utah border on U.S. 50

Sept. 12: 70.2 miles
- 5 miles east of Nevada/Utah border on U.S. 50
- 20 miles west of Delta, Utah on U.S. 50

Sept. 13: 60 miles
- 20 miles west of Delta on U.S. 50
- To 45 miles west of Provo, Utah on Route 6

Sept. 14: 60.7 miles
- 45 miles west of Provo on Route 6
- To Santaquin, Utah on Route 6
- Left onto Route 198
- To right on 400 West in Payson, Utah

- To left on South State Road which become Route 89
- To left on East 300 Street
- To right on Route 189
- To 6 miles east of Provo on East Provo Canyon Road (Route 189)

Sept. 15: 64.8 miles
- 6 miles east of Provo on East Provo Canyon Road (Route 189)
- To right on U.S. 40 in Heber City, Utah
- To 5 miles west of Fruitland, Utah on U.S. 40

Sept. 16: 68.1 miles
- 5 miles west of Fruitland on U.S. 40
- To 9 miles east of Vernal, Utah on U.S. 40

Sept. 17: 63.8 miles
- 9 miles west of Fruitland on U.S. 40
- To 3 miles west of Massadona, Colorado on U.S. 40

Sept. 18: 68 miles
- 3 miles west of Massadona on U.S. 40
- To Craig, Colorado on U.S. 40

Sept. 19: 62.4 miles
- Craig on U.S. 40
- To 22 miles east of Steamboat Springs, Colorado on U.S. 40

Sept. 20: 62.5 miles
- 22 miles east of Steamboat Springs on U.S. 40
- To 27 miles east of Walden, Colorado on Route 14

Sept. 21: 70.6 miles
- 27 miles east of Walden on Route 14
- To junction of Colorado 14 and Colorado 287 just west of Fort Collins, Colorado

Sept. 22: 70.6 miles
- Junction of Colorado 14 and Colorado 287 just west of Fort Collins
- Right turn onto Colorado 14 through Fort Collins
- To Raymer, Colorado on Colorado 14

Sept. 23: 62 miles
- Raymer, Colorado on Colorado 14
- To left at junction of U.S. 138
- To 4 miles east of Crook Colorado on U.S. 138

Sept, 24: 63.2 miles
- 4 miles east of Crook, Colorado on U.S. 138
- Stay on U.S. 138 to Big Springs, Colorado
- Continue on U.S. 138
- To junction U.S. 30, turn right onto U.S. 30

- To 1 mile east of Ogallala, Nebraska on U.S. 30

Sept. 25: 65.6 miles
- 1 mile east of Ogallala on U.S. 30
- Stay on U.S. 30 thru North Platte, Nebraska
- To Maxwell, Nebraska on U.S. 30

Sept. 26: 64.8 miles
- Maxwell, Nebraska on U.S. 30
- To 5 miles west of Elm Creek, Nebraska on U.S. 30

Sept. 27: 70 miles
- 5 miles west of Elm Creek, Nebraska on U.S. 30
- To east of Grand Island, Nebraska

Sept. 28: 70 miles
- East of Grand Island, Nebraska
- Onto U.S. 34
- To west of Lincoln, Nebraska on U.S. 34

Sept. 29: 65 miles
- West of Lincoln on U.S. 34
- To left on Superior Street
- To left onto Route 6 to Omaha, Nebraska
- To right on West Dodge Street (Route 6)
- Through downtown Omaha on Dodge Street (Route 6)
- To the bridge across Missouri River on I-480 (aka Route 6)

Sept. 30: 72.6 miles
- On I-480 in Omaha across the bridge over the Missouri River
- Thru Council Bluffs, Iowa on Route 6
- Stay on Route 6 thru Oakland, Iowa and thru Atlantic, Iowa
- Onto White Pole Road (Route 83)
- To Anita, Iowa on Route 83

Oct. 1: 70 miles
- Anita on Route 83
- Through Anita
- Onto White Pole Road to Dexter, Iowa
- To south on Eldorado Avenue
- To left on 105th Street
- To left on Kiowa Avenue
- To right on 360th Street
- Onto Grand Avenue
- Through downtown on Grand Avenue over the Des Moines River
- Onto Hubbell Avenue (Route 6)
- To east of Des Moines, Iowa by Adventureland Amusement Park on U.S. 65

Oct. 2: 71 miles
- East of Des Moines by Adventureland on U.S. 65
- On NE Hubbell Avenue
- To right on NE 70th Avenue
- Onto South 12th Avenue West
- To left on West 126th Street North
- To right on North 19th Avenue West
- To south on West 28th Street North
- to south on Route 14
- to left on Route 6 through Newton, Iowa
- through Grinnell, Iowa on Route 6
- To 15 miles east of Grinnell on Route 6

Oct. 3: 70 miles
- 15 miles east of Grinnell, Iowa on Route 6
- Through Iowa City on Route 6
- To west of Wilton, Iowa on Route 6

Oct. 4: 72 miles
- Through the Quad Cities and over the Mississippi River
- West of Wilton, Iowa on Route 6
- To right on West 5th Street
- To Durant, Iowa
- To Walcott, Iowa on 200th Street
- To Route 6
- To Hickory Grove Road
- To left on West Locust Street
- To south on North Harrison Street
- To right on East River Drive
- To left on Route 67 across bridge over the Mississippi
- To 17th Street which becomes 24th Street to left on Route 5 (Blackhawk Road)
- To Rock Island Milan Parkway
- To left on Airport Road to 69th Avenue to 27th Street onto Route 6
- To Mineral, Illinois on Route 6

Oct. 5: 70 miles
- Mineral, Illinois, on Route 6
- Through LaSalle, Illinois, on Route 6
- Through Ottawa, Illinois on Route 6
- To left on East North Drive
- To right on North 30th Road to Morris Road to Marseilles Road to Route 6 east of Marseilles, Illinois

Oct. 6: 70 miles
- East of Marseilles, Illinois on Route 6
- To Joliet, Illinois, on Route 6
- To U.S. 30 in Joliet

- To just east of Chicago Heights, Illinois over the Illinois-Indiana border on U.S. 30

Oct. 7: 70 miles
- East of the Illinois-Indiana border on U.S. 30
- To east of Bourbon, Indiana on U.S. 30

Oct. 8: 70 miles
- East of Bourbon, Indiana on U.S. 30
- To east of Fort Wayne, Indiana, near Indiana- Ohio border on U.S. 30

Oct. 9: 72 miles
- East of Fort Wayne, Indiana on U.S. 30
- To U.S. 224
- To west of Findlay, Ohio on U.S. 224

Oct. 10: 73.4 miles
- West of Findlay, Ohio on U.S. 224
- To east of Greenwich, Ohio on U.S. 224

Oct. 11: 72.3 miles
- East of Greenwich, Ohio on U.S. 224
- South of Akron, Ohio on U.S. 224
- To west of Deerfield, Ohio on U.S. 224
-

Oct. 12: 73 miles
- To west of Deerfield on U.S. 224
- Through Boardman, Ohio, on U.S. 224
- To New Castle, Pennsylvania on U.S. 224
- To west of Butler, Pennsylvania on U.S. 224

Oct. 13: 82 miles
- West of Butler, Pennsylvania on U.S. 224
- To U.S. 422
- To west of Kittanning, Pennsylvania on U.S. 422
- To Franklin Hill Road
- To Butler Road
- To Clearfield Pike (Route 85)
- To left on U.S. 119
- To west of Marion Center
- Through Marion Center on Main Street
- To right on Decker's Point Road
- To right on Julick Road
- To left on Pine Vale Road
- To right on Rairigh Road
- To left on Walker Road
- To right on Snyder Road
- To right on Shields Road
- To left on Wilgus Road

- To right on Upper Wilgus Road
- To left on Rod and Gun Club Road
- To right on Number Eleven Road
- To left on Route 286
- To right on Arcadia Road
- To left on Peles Road
- To right on Pearce Road
- To Clark Road
- To right on Benzie Road
- To right on Rock Run Road
- To left on Kantz Hill Road
- To right on Patchin Highway
- To right on Solley Road
- To left on Harmony Road
- To right on Ridge Road
- To left on Westover Road which becomes West Bridge Street
- To east of Westover, Pennsylvania on Westover Road

Oct. 14: 73.4 miles
- East of Westover, Pennsylvania on Westover Road
- To Pumpkin Ridge Road
- To Barrens Road
- Left on St. Lawrence Road
- To right on Church Hill Road
- To left on Beaver Valley Road
- Right on Glendale Valley Road
- Left on Roseland Road
- Onto Executive Drive (Route 253)
- Onto Cambria Street (Route 253)
- Right on Viola Pike (Route 453)
- Onto Janesville Pike (Route 453)
- Onto West 15th Street (Route 453) through Tyrone, Pennsylvania
- Right on Lincoln Avenue (Route 453)
- Left on West 14th (Route 453)
- Right on Pennsylvania Avenue (Route 453)
- Left on 11th Street (Route 453)
- Onto Birmingham Pike (Route 453)
- Left onto Pennington Road (Truck Route 45)
- To Center Line Road through Frogtown
- Left on Center Line Road to right through Spring Mount
- Onto Half Moon Valley Road (U.S. 550)
- Onto West Buffalo Run Road (U.S. 550)
- To right onto U.S. 322 through State College, Pennsylvania
- To east of State College on U.S. 322

Oct. 15: 73.8 miles
- East of State College on U.S. 322
- To left onto Earlystown Road (Route 45)
- On Penns Valley Road (Route 45)

- Onto Old Turnpike Road (Route 45)
- Through Mifflinburg, Pennsylvania (Route 45)
- Through Lewisburg, Pennsylvania (Route 45)
- Right on Susquehanna Trail (Route 147)
- To left on Water Street (Route 11)
- Through Danville, Pennsylvania (Route 11)
- Through Bloomsburg, Pennsylvania (Route 11)
- To west of Berwick, Pennsylvania on Route 11

Oct. 16: 73.8 miles
- West of Berwick, Pennsylvania on Route 11
- Onto West Front Street in Berwick on Route 11
- Right on Route 93 thru Nescopek, Pennsylvania
- Bear right onto Berwick-Hazelton Highway (Route 93)
- Thru Hazelton, Pennsylvania on Route 93
- Onto Susquehanna Boulevard (Route 93) continuing through Hazelton
- Stay on Route 93 to left on U.S. 209
- Stay on 299 passed Jim Thorpe, Pennsylvania
- Left on Forge Street in Lehighton, Pennsylvania (Route 299)
- Right onto Route 248
- Stay on and bear right and continue on Route 248 (Lehigh Drive)
- Onto Pheasant Drive (Route 248)
- Through Bath, Pennsylvania (Route 248)
- Thru Nazareth, Pennsylvania (Route 248)
- To west of Easton, Pensylvania

Oct. 17: 73.6 miles
- West of Easton, Pennsylvania on Route 248
- Left onto Route 22
- Thru Easton, Pennsylvania on Route 22
- Across the Delaware River into New Jersey on Route 22
- Through Phillipsburg, New Jersey onto Memorial Highway (Route 22)
- Onto Route 173 through Bloomsbury, New Jersey
- Bear right stay on Route 173 into Clinton, New Jersey
- Onto Old Highway 22 through Clinton, New Jersey
- Onto Route 31 going east through Clinton, New Jersey
- Left onto Beaver Street through Clinton, New Jersey
- On Beaver Street onto Beaver Avenue onto Route 22
- Stay on Route 22 through Lebanon/ Bridgewater/ Somerset/ Middlesex/ Dunellen/North Plainfield, New Jersey
- To right on Park Avenue in Scotch Plains, New Jersey
- Onto North Martine Avenue
- Left on South Avenue (Route 28)
- To North Avenue East (Route 28) through Garwood/Cranfield, New Jersey
- Onto West Wesfield Avenue in Roselle, New Jersey
- Onto East Westfield Avenue in Roselle, New Jersey

- Right onto Elmora Avenue in Elizabeth, New Jersey
- Onto South Elmora Avenue in Elizabeth, New Jersey
- Onto Bayway Avenue in Elizabeth, New Jersey
- Over the Goethals Bridge (I-278) with Elizabeth Police Department escort
- Onto Staten Island Expressway (I-278)
- To the official finish of the Run Across America at the Verrazano-Narrows Bridge toll plaza in Staten Island, New York
  Guinness World Record claim: San Francisco City Hall to Verrazano-Narrows Bridge toll plaza in Staten Island, New York
  3,103 miles: 46 days, 8 hours, 36 minutes

Oct. 18: 9.9 miles
Ceremonial finish on the Brooklyn Bridge and at City Hall, New York City
- New York Police Department escort from Staten Island toll plaza (on I-278) across the lower level on the Verrazano-Narrows Bridge into Brooklyn, New York
- Onto 4th Avenue in Brooklyn
- Left on Atlantic Avenue in Brooklyn
- Right on Adams Street in Brooklyn
- Onto the Brooklyn Bridge for brief ceremony
- Onto City Hall Park and the steps of City Hall for the end of the ceremonial finish

Kevin Gleason has been a writer and editor since graduating from SUNY Plattsburgh three decades ago. He has won dozens of state and national writing awards, and he is currently sports editor of the *Times Herald-Record*, a mid-sized daily newspaper in Middletown, New York. Kevin spends most of his free time cheering on his two beautiful children, Gabrielle, 14, and Dillon, 13, in their various sporting endeavors.

***

For additional copies of *46 Days* or to arrange a book signing:
- Email Kevin at kgleasonthr@yahoo.com or Frank at frankg@shoe-fitter.com
- Call Frank at 845-551-8270 or visit him at Frank's Custom Shoe Fitting, 329 Route 211, Middletown, NY 10940

46 Days is also available at RecordBreakingRun.com and on Amazon.com

Made in the USA
Lexington, KY
31 March 2017